HOW TO READ THE GOSPELS

PETER SCHMIDT

How to read the
GOSPELS

Historicity and truth in the
Gospels and Acts

ST PAULS

Original title: *Woord Van God – Boek van Mensen*
© Uitgeverij Altiona-Averbode, Belgium 1990

Translated by C. Vanhove-Romanik, STL

St Pauls
Middlegreen, Slough SL3 6BT, United Kingdom
Moyglare Road, Maynooth, Co. Kildare, Ireland

English translation © St Pauls 1993

ISBN 085439 430 3

Printed by The Guernsey Press Co. Ltd, Guernsey, C.I.

St Pauls is an activity of the priests and brothers of the Society of St Paul who proclaim the Gospel through the media of social communication

Contents

Books of the Bible:

Gen	Genesis	Mt	Matthew
Ex	Exodus	Mk	Mark
Lev	Leviticus	Lk	Luke
Num	Numbers	Jn	John
Dt	Deuteronomy	Acts	Acts of the Apostles
Josh	Joshua	Rom	Romans
Judg	Judges	1 Cor	1 Corinthians
1 Sam	1 Samuel	2 Cor	2 Corinthians
2 Sam	2 Samuel	Gal	Galatians
1 Chron	1 Chronicles	Eph	Ephesians
2 Chron	2 Chronicles	Phil	Philippians
Ps	Psalms	Col	Colossians
Prov	Proverbs	1 Thess	1 Thessalonians
Eccles	Ecclesiastes	2 Thess	2 Thessalonians
Is	Isaiah	1 Tim	1 Timothy
Jer	Jeremiah	2 Tim	2 Timothy
Lam	Lamentations	Tit	Titus
Ezek	Ezekiel	Philem	Philemon
Dan	Daniel	Heb	Hebrews
Hos	Hosea	Jas	James
Obad	Obadiah	1 Pet	1 Peter
Jon	Jonah	2 Pet	2 Peter
Mic	Micah	1 Jn	1 John
Hab	Habakkuk	2 Jn	2 John
Zeph	Zephaniah	3 Jn	3 John
Hag	Haggai	Rev	Revelation (Apocalipse)
Zech	Zechariah		
Mal	Malachi		
Sir	Sirach (Ecclesiasticus)		

Books, Series and Periodicals:

AB	Anchor Bible
BETL	Bibliothecarum Ephemeridum Theologicarum Lovaniensium
Cah.Év.	Cahiers Évangéliques

DDB	Desclée de Brouwer
EKKNT	Evangelisch-Katholischer Kommentar zum Neuen Testament
FRLANT	Forschungen zur Religion und Literatur des Alten und Neuen Testaments
HTKNT	Herders Theologischer Kommentar zum Neuen Testament
ThHKNT	Theologischer Handkommentar zum Neuen Testament

Other:

art. cit.	the article referred to
cf	confer
ch.	chapter
col(l).	column(s)
cp	compare
e.g.	for example
f	following verse
ff	following verses
ms(s).	manuscript(s)
n.	note
op. cit.	the book referred to
par.	parallel(s)
s.v.	sub voce = under the word
SgLk	Sondergut Luke
SgMk	Sondergut Mark
SgMt	Sondergut Matthew
SgJn	Sondergut John
v.	verse
vv.	verses
vol	volume
//	parallel
[]	author's comment, when present in a quotation translation, when following a foreing language title

Introduction

The introduction to the gospels and Acts offered here is the first part of an introduction to the whole New Testament. In writing this introduction we have relied heavily on material written earlier: a 'theme book' for theological conferences for priests of the diocese of Ghent (1987-1988) and unpublished course material composed for a series of public lectures in the diocese of Ghent (1988-1989). The advantage of this is that many examples and explanations have already been tested 'in the field'.

In composing this introduction we have been led by one conscious purpose. Teaching courses for a general public has shown us that many people who have wanted to know more about Scripture have felt hindered by the difficult problem of 'historical reality' and the 'gospel's truth'; or put more simply, between what 'really happened' and what 'is true'. 'Are these stories to be believed?' or conversely, 'If that didn't really happen either, what are we supposed to believe of what's left? What bag of goods have they sold us?...' This and similar problems may well have been surpassed long ago by professional exegetes and theologians, for non-specialists they still form a stumbling block, often difficult to remove, when reading the Scriptures. We have written this introduction to the gospels and Acts with the express intention of explaining the relationship between historicity and truth in the New Testament in a way accessible to all. In so doing we hope to remove a number of superfluous but hindersome obstacles and to help potential Scripture readers in their first contacts with the text. This concern has determined the content and structure of the book. It makes no attempt to develop directly methods for reading, nor to provide a history of the New Testament era, nor to outline the cultural background of the period. It wishes to guide the reader on a brief exploration of the unique characteristics of the gospel literature providing an insight in the above mentioned problem. We are really saying, 'Look, this is what you need to know first when, as a modern believer who also wants to remain an intelligent thinking person, you take the gospel in hand.'

The first chapter explains that the gospel is also, unavoidably, a particular literary genre requiring its own keys to interpretation. Before we look at the gospel's own genre, the second chapter demonstrates the importance of history for the Bible; in particular, the importance of Jesus' own factuality for the structure of Christian faith. Although this second chapter is important as a basis for the main idea of the book, it has the form of an *excursus*. It can be passed over in a first reading to be examined more closely later on. The third chapter discusses the path the teaching about Jesus followed before it reached its final form in our present gospels. The fourth chapter treats the synoptic question. Because we are convinced of the importance of an insight into this question for a more correct insight into the gospels, we have not limited ourselves to the current dominant view. We try to lead the reader along in the problems and reasoning which led to the two-source theory. We do this having had the experience that the non-specialist is quite able to follow the essential points of the question. Moreover, it offers a firm footing when the reader can see that the present theses on the development of the gospels and their interrelationship are well grounded. Finally, chapters five to eight treat the evangelists individually, each with his own characteristics. Acts has been included when treating Luke.

At regular intervals certain parts of the text have been enclosed between the graphic signs ≥ … ≤. This indicates that this part of the text – sometimes a paragraph, sometimes a few pages – is particularly suitable for use as a reading exercise or for practical application in the context of a Bible study group or for an evening of study and prayer. Indeed, the book is also intended as a guide for Bible study groups and their leaders. This implies that the book is read most profitably with the Bible open beside it. It is essential to take the time to read serenely the many biblical references in order to follow all the explanations easily.

This introduction is expressly intended for non-specialists. In this sense too, it is an introduction. To avoid over-taxing the text with data useful only for professionals, the number of notes and references have been limited to the essential minimum. In addition, a number of technical terms have been explained when they could not be avoided. The notes have, as a result, often an explanatory function.

Quotations from the Bible in this English edition come from *Revised Standard Version*. When texts are compared, the English is also guided by the layout of the (Dutch language) synopsis prepared by A. Devaux and M. Vervenne.

The Author

1

The gospel as literary genre

A note on interpreting and ways of expressing the truth

People are beings who hunger for truth. The search for truth is one of their most fundamental characteristics; Pilate's question forms a driving force in the history of human thought and behaviour. In all its speaking and writing, humanity attempts in one way or another to express truth. The fact that in nearly all areas of knowledge and behaviour it knows it is still far from the truth, that it is often confronted with lies and deception, that it sometimes even doubts whether it will ever be able to know the truth and despairingly wonders what the truth really is, all this in no way diminishes its fundamental orientation. On the contrary, even the denial or twisting of the truth is still a form of its affirmation; concepts such as 'lying', 'speaking falsely' and 'being mistaken' are only meaningful against a contrasting background of faith in the truth. This book does not intend to treat the problem of truth formally. We wish only to illustrate that it is no accident when people closely associate concepts such as revelation and faith with the search for truth and when believers consider the Holy Scripture an extremely important expression of truth. They even see it as a gift of God in which they find a guide to thinking and acting 'according to the truth'. Speaking very generally, we could say that in one way or another the believer expects the Scriptures to offer him truth.

What we call 'truth' is so rich that we approach and express it from thousands of directions. No single human concept or word expresses all aspects of the truth at the same time. We never see truth to us as an indivisible, monolithic block, but always in an inexhaustibly rich variety of layers and patterns of meaning. We wish by no means to imply that truth as such can be ambivalent or even contradictory, nor do we defend the principle of 'each his own truth'. Rather, it is our conviction that only one truth can exist and that it comprises all of reality. But it would be naive to think that people can circumscribe this totality and express it free of all aspects. Our ways to approach the truth and forms to express it vary endlessly.

There are mathematical approaches to truth alongside poetical, moral alongside juridical, esthetical alongside historical, and so on. Paul's image of the body and its many members could well be applied to the human approach to truth. Although all members and organs compose the one body, the eye's function differs from that of the nose, and the lungs' from the liver's... It is the same with the human expression of truth. The function of the biological expression of truth does not coincide with the poetical, nor the historiographic with the religious. The multiplicity of approaches to and expressions of truth is undoubtedly related to the limitations of the human mind. We are unable to approach and express truth absolutely and without predisposition. We look and think in fragments and try, with effort, to compose the whole picture of the mosaic of truth by laying out its many small stones. But we could also say that it belongs to the richness of the human spirit that people are able to bring to expression the many layers and domains of truth in such a varied manner.

All this brings us immediately to the important problem of *interpretation* and *hermeneutics*.[1] When someone wants to grasp the unique nuances of the truth of a word or expression, he has to interpret correctly. This requires first of all that within the range of possible meanings he finds just *that* one intended by the word or expression. This is now we speak every day. Spontaneously and generally without conscious reflection, we grasp the proper level of truth of the words because we interpret them in a different way as the need arises. We understand spontaneously that the expression 'John has a heart of gold' lies on another level of meaning than 'John has a golden ring'. When someone refers to 'those poor old oil sheiks' we understand spontaneously the use of irony. The intended truth lies diametrically opposite the word used. These two examples are obvious; if the meaning of the words is sought in the wrong field of interpretation, then the intended truth will not be understood. We have struck out. It is worth the effort to examine consciously this continuous, nearly unconscious game our minds play. How is it that we understand the difference between what is literally intended and imagery? Why do we understand figures of style, plays on words, ambiguity and irony? How do we know something is being kept back, that we have to read 'between the lines'?... It is amazing how numerous and complex our permanent changes of level are. Every reader understands spontaneously the figurative meaning of the expression used above 'to strike out'. The truth of this expression lies in another context than when it is used during a baseball game and must therefore be sought on another level. Human language continually jumps from the one level of meaning to another. This allows us to speak of 'screaming colours' and 'dark sounds'. It is the whole play of multiple meanings: poetry, metaphor, comparison, word play, humour, symbolism... Yet this ceaseless jumping from one level of meaning to another is not a talent inherited at birth. It must be learned! This is the reason why children take stories so literally, why they are so easily deceived, or why a six-year old child cannot understand irony or word play. It all belongs to the long process of learning to interpret. It is still possible at any age to misjudge the level of meaning; that is why someone can be fooled or cheated, why people misunderstand texts and why misunderstandings and mistakes remain possible.

The same situation holds true for written language. No single text expresses in one go all aspects of the truth. A novel must be read differently from the report of a parliamentary session, and a poem is not an historical reconstruction. Whoever reads Gezelle's verse 'I am a flower, and blossom in Your sight...' from the point of view of a course in botany seriously risks missing the point of the poem! The rule in literature is thus: *different types of writing require different types of interpretation.* And also: *a different approach to truth requires a different way of writing.*

From a reporter we expect correctly an exact representation

of facts and words, and the *truth* of his report will, for the most part, be directly proportional with its *accuracy*. Such accuracy is not required of a novelist, which does not mean that a novelist is unable to pass on truth. How many lessons have we not learned from *Don Quixote* or *The Brothers Karamazov*! But the novel expresses truth *in another way* than the report, the novel belongs to *another literary genre*.

The Holy Scriptures do not escape this pattern. This is an essential part of its human character. The Bible was written by people and is also read and understood by people. There is no single scriptural text where *the* truth is expressed in a nutshell. The unique value of a scriptural text cannot be found on all levels, and *without interpretation* it cannot be brought to light. We often hear the question, why make it so difficult? Why not just read what is written? However well intended, these and similar questions point to a too naively spontaneous approach to the text. The problem is, 'just reading what is written' is impossible. What is written is never *only* what is written there. A text or an event must *always* be interpreted in order to be understood! This is one of the most unavoidable aspects of the relationship between reality and the human knowledge of the expression of truth. Moreover, interpretation always involves choosing from among various possible levels of meaning offered within a given context or situation. This choice can be correct or incorrect, but interpretation cannot be avoided. When, for example, I see a car crash against a tree and shout 'There's an accident!', I have already interpreted the event. Strictly speaking, it could be something else: a film scene, suicide... I cannot observe an accident without interpretation. This rule is proper to the relationship between language and reality and therefore is also valid for the Holy Scriptures. Believers are generally not aware that expressions such as 'a miracle has occurred' is always founded on an interpretation of the reality.

In writing such an expression the speaker has already accepted that a God exists and that in one way or another he intervenes in the events of this world. Calling an unexplainable healing a miracle does not itself prove the existence of God, but is rather the result of accepting God's existence, accepting a number of ideas about God bound to it, and the interpretation of events in the light of these ideas about God.

Every human word must be interpreted in order to be understood. This is also the case when, as Jews and Christians believe, this human word is the vehicle for truth come from God. After a long history of interpretation often troubled by painful misunderstandings, the Church has accepted that the Scripture has its own *specific domain of truth*. It is not that of biology or physics, not that of economics or politics, not even that of history as such. In Scripture we are concerned with the level of truth that relates to the relationship between God and his people. Put differently, the level of truth as *saving truth*.

Since the end of the nineteenth century, we have known that knowledge of the various *literary genres* plays a very important role in the interpretation of the Old Testament. Until rather recently, the stories in the Old Testament were read more or less as an historical report; everything mentioned in the Bible was uncritically accepted as having 'really happened' and the truth of God's revelation was made contingent on this 'really having happened'. This method of interpretation not only led to the most bizarre 'scientific' research,[2] but also played an important role in dramatic conflicts such as those surrounding Galileo and Darwin.[3] People were not yet aware that the biblical view of the world was very much bound up in its own time and culture, and could make no claim to scientific authority. Similarly, the various language levels were all treated the same so that symbolic or metaphorical language was often interpreted in the same way as historical or scientific language. One of the great merits of what has been called source criticism[4] since the nineteenth century was that it made people aware of the rich variety of *literary genres* in the Bible – saga, legend, song, aphorism, historical chronicle, letter, oracle... – each with its own characteristics and levels of meaning. The exegesis and theology of the last two centuries have taught us to understand that 'really happened' and 'true' are not necessarily congruent concepts. The proper situation and intention – and thus the limits! – of a text must always be tested so that its own 'truth' will come to light. Far from being detrimental to the believability and authority of the

Scriptures, these liberating insights have removed many useless stumbling blocks and greatly advanced and deepened the faithfilled reading of the Scriptures.

The same observation is true of the New Testament. There, too, various forms of expression play a role. The New Testament, as the Old, cannot be understood without some form of hermeneutics. Paul's letters belong clearly to another genre than the Acts of the Apostles which, in its turn, must be read differently than the Apocalypse. There is even a difference in genre among the various letters, the letter to the Hebrews is very different from Paul's letter to his friend Philemon. *The gospels also form a separate literary genre.* Even more, within one and the same gospel, various genres can be found side by side. A parable has to be interpreted differently from the passion narrative, and one of Jesus' prophetic discourses differs from a dispute. Even within the separate genres we must distinguish between categories requiring different treatment. Within the genre of miracle stories, the nature miracles have many aspects requiring a different interpretation from the miracles of healing. A responsible reading of the gospel texts must continually take this into consideration. The New Testament also presents the unavoidable problems of every interpretation. Whoever errs in genre or intention risks missing the point of the story, the specific truth of the text. We are therefore faced with the question, what sort of book is a gospel? What sort of truth does a gospel try to convey and how does it express it? Should a reference to Jesus 'walking across water' be understood on the same level as Jesus 'walking across the temple square'? Or, as W. Luypen wrotes is the expression 'Christ rose from his grave' on the same level as 'Chris rose from his beach chair'?[5]

In the following pages we present several elements which can help the reader to discover the unique literary genre of the gospel.

The gospel is neither a news report, nor a biography, nor a memoir

≥ Let us begin our search for the character of a gospel with a pleasant and instructive exercise. We put on Sherlock Holmes' hat and presuppose we have been given the task of drawing up the most accurate possible historical reconstruction of the events around Jesus and the words he spoke. The inspiration of the Holy Spirit guarantees a faultless transmission of the events and words. Given the same inspiration, the same principle holds true for the Acts of the Apostles. With these premises in mind and magnifying glass in hand, we examine a few texts which appear useful for the purpose of an exact reconstruction.

We compare:
– Mk 15:25 with Jn 19:14. At what time exactly was Jesus crucified? According to Mark, Jesus hung on the cross at 9 am (the third hour of the ancient division of hours) while, according to John, he still stood before Pilate around noon (the sixth hour). They cannot both be right. Why then do they give such precise indications of time?
– Mt 26:17-19 (cf Mk 14:12-16 and Lk 22:7-15) with John 18:28. Was the Last Supper a passover meal or not? If so, how can John write that on Good Friday the Jews still had 'to eat the passover'?
– Mt 27:1-10 with Acts 1:16-20. What really happened with the money? Did Judas throw it away and did the high priests buy the potter's field with it to bury strangers? Or did Judas himself buy the field 'with the reward of his wickedness'? Both texts refer to the same 'field of blood', do they not?
– Lk 23:26 with Jn 19:17. Is it Simon of Cyrene who carried the cross behind Jesus or did Jesus himself carry his cross to Golgotha?
– Mt 27:44 with Lk 23:39-43. Did both thieves taunt Jesus or was it only one, while the other asked for mercy?
– Mt 28:7-10 and Mc 16:7 with Lk 24:49 and Acts 1:4. What exactly was Jesus' command after his resurrection? Were

the disciples to go to Galilee, or were they forbidden to leave Jerusalem until after Pentecost?

– Lk 24 (note carefully the references to time in vv. 1, 13, 29, 33, 36, 44, 50!) with Acts 1:3-12. When did Jesus ascend to heaven? After 40 days, according to Acts, or on Easter itself as the precise chronological references in Luke 24 presuppose? Or did he bid farewell in Galilee, as the end of Matthew's gospel suggests?

– Mk 5:1ff with Mt 8:28ff. Where did the healing take place? Near Gadara or Gerasa? How many possessed were there, one or two? Both versions refer to the same exorcism story with the herd of pigs!

– Mt 1:6-16 with Lk 3:23-31. Who was the father of Joseph, Eli or Jacob? From which of David's sons does Jesus descend, Solomon or Nathan? Compare the rest of the two genealogies, there are many discrepancies.

– Mk 11:15-19 with Jn 2:13-16. When did the cleansing of the temple take place? At the start of Jesus' public life, two or three years before his death – according to John – or at the very end, a few days before his death – according to Mark?

– Lk 1:26; 2:4,39 with Mt 2:19-23. Did Joseph and Mary already live in Nazareth before Jesus was born, as Luke says or did they settle there only after their return from Egypt as Matthew writes? How do we harmonize the flight to Egypt (Mt 2) with the idea of Lk 2:39 according to which Joseph and Mary returned to Nazareth after they had 'performed everything according to the law'?

– Mk 2:13-14; 4:35-41 with Mt 8:23-27; 9:9-10. Was the tax collector called before or after the storm on the sea?

These are just a dozen examples, haphazardly chosen. This list can easily be extended with a few dozen more. E.g. what were Jesus' exact words when he formulated the beatitudes (cf Mt 5:3-12 with Lk 6:20-26) and the consecration words of the Eucharist at the Last Supper (cf Mt 26:26-29 with Mk 14:22-25, Lk 22:15-22 and 1 Cor 11:23-25)? What happened exactly at the discovery of the empty tomb and the appearances of the risen Jesus (cf Mt 28; Mk 16:1-8; Lk 24; Jn 20-21; 1 Cor 15:3-

7)? What was the exact text on the sign above the cross (cf Mt 27:37 with Mk 15:26; Lk 23:38; Jn 19:19)? When forbidding divorce did Jesus really say, 'except on the ground of unchastity...' (cf Mt 5:32; 19:5 with Mk 10:9-12; if Jesus said this why does Mark omit it, and if not, why did Matthew add it)? And so on. ≤

These examples speak for themselves. Whoever tries to approach the gospels solely from the question, 'what exactly was done and said?', and then studies the texts closely soon finds himself tangled in insurmountable difficulties. We see immediately the kinds of problems that arise when the gospel's truth is tightly bound to precise historical reconstruction. Believing without difficulty in the possibility of an accurate and exact reconstruction of the facts is possible only for those unfamiliar with the matter, i.e. for those who read the texts only superficially or who neglect comparing them to one another. The so-called 'synoptic question'[6] had demonstrated even in the last century that an exact biography of Jesus is impossible. Throughout the nineteenth century biblical scholars and theologians worked laboriously to remove Jesus 'from under the dust of dogma and ecclesiastical tradition' and to reconstruct his figure in its historical purity. This attempt failed because it was discovered that an image of Jesus free of all Church interpretation could not be extracted.[7] The reason for this will be explained further on in this book. The 'Lives of Jesus' are all the result of harmonizing the gospel texts during which process all disturbing rough spots or contradictions are either eliminated or are explained in a forced way. The procedure of 'harmonizing the gospels' is very old. It has been practiced since the second century. The oldest known attempt to harmonize the gospels is known as the *Diatessaron* of the Syrian, Tatian. This was a book in which the four gospels were woven into one continuous story. (The Greek word *diatessaron* means literally 'by means of the four'.) The harmonization procedure has always dominated catechesis, devotion and liturgy. For example, the liturgy for Christmas is based on an – exegetically impossible – harmonization of the infancy narratives in Matthew and Luke. Seen from an educational point of view this is no disaster and in a certain way we could say that devotion and liturgy are correct, because they unconsciously put the gospel's level of truth on a different plane than that of exact historical reconstruction. Yet from the beginning of the modern period this harmonization procedure has raised problems. The Christians' general and spontaneous conviction regarding 'Bible history' was determined by a 'polished' reading of the gospels which lost sight of the divergences and contradictions among the original texts. When from the sixteenth century onward – following the humanists' interest in the original texts as well as the renewed interest in the Bible encouraged by the Reformation – the gospels were given a more critical glance, the difficulties became apparent. In the seventeenth century and even more in the eighteenth, when the Enlightenment exerted its influence on biblical research, the problems grew. Unresolvable differences were discovered and openly discussed. This critical reading clashed with the generally accepted conviction that the infallible truth of the gospels was guaranteed by the absolute historical correctness of all the events and words transmitted. The tension between the critical reading of the gospels and the Church's spontaneous image which was considered sacrosanct, encouraged many erroneous and useless apologetic efforts. Very often people marshalled all efforts to prove things which in fact lie outside the possibilities of historical verification, and which even lie outside the specific horizon of the gospels.

The examples listed above of 'static' in the gospel texts lead us to suspect that a gospel *must be read differently from a pure, factual account.* First they show that, in any case, the idea of 'the inspiration of the Holy Spirit' cannot mean that God will have seen to it that the gospels contain not one historical irregularity. What the Church calls 'the inspiration of the Holy Spirit' is no substitute for human methodology or for the restrictions on human memories. Variations arising spontaneously during oral transmission can also be found in the gospels. Moreover, the evangelists were neither 'great' writers nor scientific researchers. Their writing is occasionally somewhat clumsy, they not only make grammatical faults but there is no doubt that they also are subject to historical inaccuracies and errors.

There is more. We do not do the gospels justice when we limit their interpretation to the level of historical exactitude, and bind to this the truth they contain. A gospel is a *very singular type of book*. It forms its very own *genre*. This singularity can be formulated negatively: although the gospel contains much historical material and may be included in the category historical literature, it is not a history book; although it contains many accurate recollections, it cannot justly be classified in the genre memoirs; although it relates many accurate facts, it is not a report or a factual account; although many biographical elements are met there, and even though taken as a whole it has the form of a biographical narrative, it is still not a biography.

At this stage in our explanation we cannot yet give a positive outline of the genre gospel. Before we can do this we have to review a whole list of historical and literary questions. But very generally we can say that the evangelists were not really interested in writing a biography of Jesus, or in collecting material that would allow later generations of Christians to reconstruct events and words accurately. The gospels contain only a very small part of all that Jesus said and did – a gospel is really a very small book! What the evangelists wanted was in the first place to write a book that *contains and transmits Jesus' good news about the kingdom of God*. That good news is what we call 'The Good News', in Greek *euangelion*, from which our word evangelist is derived. The evangelists were concerned with proclaiming that Jesus is the Messiah. In a manner of speaking, they wrote down not one single word or fact from purely 'neutral' historical interest. Everything in the gospel is coloured by a *believing interpretation* of the events around Jesus and is in service of the invitation to faith, where 'faith' refers not so much to the intellectual acceptance of 'truths', but rather to a life-long commitment to the imitation of Christ. In other words, an evangelist does not want a reader to finish reading the gospel and then say, 'Now I know what happened in Jesus' life', but rather, 'Truly, this Jesus of Nazareth is the Christ, the Lord. To him will I listen. He is the one I will follow'. The evangelists' intention was to write a *book of faith*. That this influenced the very writing as well as determining the selection of facts and words is obvious. What,

25

for example, would a biographer who wanted to show in less than 100 pages that Napoleon was a belligerent megalomaniac choose from the available material? What would a biographer who wanted to highlight Napoleon's magnitude as a statesman and law-maker and to share with readers his admiration for this highly gifted figure select from this same material?... On every page the gospels want to show Jesus as the Son of God. In so doing they want to be fundamentally faithful to Jesus' life and mission, faithful to his word and work, to his death and resurrection, to his will. But they do not experience this faithfulness 'according to the letter that kills, but according to the Spirit who gives life' (2 Cor 3:6). An evangelist is not a chronicle writer. He wants to reveal Jesus' real meaning, but does not do this according to the norms of modern historical science.

A large part of this book is devoted to exploring features which allow us to localize the gospels' literary terrain, their singular level of truth. Part of this will involve following the growth of the gospel literature during the first century. The way in which the gospels came to be written teaches us much about their intention and character. The written gospels do not stand – however strange this may seem – at the start of the proclamation concerning Jesus, but characterize rather a later stage in this proclamation. The four gospels available to us are the fruit of a long tradition which underwent several phases. Before we review this evolution, we must examine a point of fundamental importance for their interpretation, namely, the relationship between history and revelation, between history and faith. We ask the question, how do the Scriptures (in our case, the gospels) themselves interpret the role of history? What importance do the gospels attribute to historical events? In other words, how do the gospels view the relationship between history and truth?

NOTES

1   The word 'hermeneutics' is the Greek equivalent of 'interpretation', which is derived from Latin. Both terms mean literally rendition. The term

'hermeneutics' (adj. hermeneutical), however, is used rather to refer to the theory or methodology of interpretation and then especially for juridical, philosophical and religious texts. Hermeneutics thus concerns the body of rules, aids and criteria for explanation.

2   From among the many scientific calculations based on a literal historical interpretation of the stories, we provide the following entertaining example as illustration. In 1679, the famous German Jesuit Athenasius Kircher published a weighty volume on the tower of Babel. He devoted a whole chapter to the problems which arise when trying to build a tower as high as heaven. He calculated that a tower reaching only as far as the moon would require 374,354,625,000,000,000 bricks of 1 cubic foot; that all the forests on earth would not supply enough fuel to bake these stones; that the weight of the tower would push the earth from its place in the center of the universe, that a rider on horseback who ascended the stairway around the tower at a rate of 30 miles a day would need more than 80 years to reach the moon, etc. According to Kircher, God was correct in punishing the people with a confusion of tongues for attempting such a senseless construction.

3   In Galileo's trial the literal astronomic interpretation of Joshua 10:12-13 played an important role. The text was to have shown that the sun revolved around the (motionless) earth and not the reverse. In the controversy around Darwin it was a question of the geological and biological interpretation of Genesis 1.

4   As the name says, 'source criticism' is the branch of biblical study whose goal is the isolation of the source material lying at the basis of a writing. When an author writes about something he has not himself seen or experienced he must have recourse to the data or documents of others. He has to have sources. These may be written (e.g. someone writes a biography and uses letters, diaries and photo albums), but also orally transmitted witnesses or traditions. Biblical source criticism has discovered that many popular or folk stories and traditions served as source material for the biblical texts.

5   W. Luypen, *Het noemen van de naam God* [*Mentioning God's Name*], Hilversum, 1980, pp. 54f.

6   See below, Chapter 4.

7   Albert Schweitzer pronounced the definitive obituary of the attempt in his still classic study *Von Reimarus zu Wrede. Die Geschichte der Leben Jesu-Forschung* [*Quest of the Historical Jesus*, London: SCM, 1981]. This does not mean that no contemporary historical research can be done regarding Jesus. On the contrary, since the Second World War we have accumulated a treasure of new historical insights which are extremely important for interpreting Jesus and his message. But the present type of historical research is very different from the compilation of a 'Life of Jesus' from harmonized gospel texts. Modern historical criticism is continually producing elements which shed light on the historical Jesus as he was before the Church's interpretation (Jesus, the Jew). However, such data must be handled very carefully, and all concrete results still show a complex, fragmentary and often strongly hypothetical image of Jesus' world. The image that the renewed historical research offers cannot be compared with the smooth, completely polished 'Lives of Jesus'. In any case, the *purely* historical description of Jesus remains only a torso.

2

History,
the place where God can be found

For the gospels, history, historical factuality, is essential. This assertion can seem to be a flagrant contradiction of the previous chapter, but that is only appearance. History is essential, not because of the highest possible accuracy in the reconstruction of facts and details, but because it determines *the singular visage of the biblical, Christian belief in revelation.*

To understand this correctly we have to step back a bit into the world view of ancient Israel, since the evangelists inherited their view of history from the Old Testament. This view thoroughly determines the structure of biblical belief. In the following paragraphs we will digress briefly from our main theme in what in a certain sense can be considered an excursus. Nevertheless, it seems useful to us to insert this explanation here, because it is important for someone who wants to read the Scriptures to have a clear understanding of the 'category history' in the Bible. Only from this can it be understood why the history of Jesus is important for faith and in what sense history, as the place where God can be found, can be a basic category for the gospels without this requiring them to be real history books.

The mythological world view is unhistorical

Simplifying somewhat but without, we hope, being incorrect we can locate the singular character of the biblical view of history by comparing it with the ancient world view of the pagan, polytheistic religions. The world view of the old pagan cultures around Israel (Egypt, Babylon, Assyria, Phoenicia) is essentially mythological.[1] A characteristic of the mythological world view is the absence of real historical awareness. This absence coincides with mythological religiosity's own nature. The basic reality in which the (pre-) philosophical religious thought of ancient cultures moves is a *sacralized world*. With this we mean that the fundamental and absolute reality which precedes all and coordinates all (philosophers speak of a transcendental reality) is the whole cosmos, the universe, the All. The cosmos (world order) is itself the real *divine reality*. This universe is higher, holier, more eternal than the personal gods. The gods themselves came into existence within the already existing 'All' reality. Even though the old polytheistic religions generally had a creating god in their pantheon (e.g. Marduk for the Babylonians, Zeus for the Greeks, El in Canaan, Khnum in Egypt) creation was still not seen as it was in the later purified biblical presentation. For the mythological religions creation meant the development and ordering of a reality which is already there, not a 'creation from nothing'. Put in theological language this means the gods are not transcendent with regard to the universe; they are not separate from it, do not rise above it, but *are a part of it*. The old myths tell not only over the *cosmogony* (how the world came to exist) but also the *theogony*, how the gods came into existence. The gods became! The gods fulfil their function within the eternal holy All just as do people, demons, animals and other beings. Their function is certainly hierarchically much higher than that of people, but essentially it is no different. Between the functions of god and human there is, in the end, only a difference of degree. The gods, who are often personifications of realities which surpass humanity (natural elements; sickness and death; fertility and sexuality; etc.), fulfil a function which *must guarantee the maintenance of the world order*. The universe revolves eternally around itself; its own organization is its goal and very meaning. All that exists within that divinity, functions in one way or another in service of the 'good order' within the universe: order of nature and of life processes; moral order, social order... Pagan religion is completely functional.

All this implies that these cultures put, as it were, divine

29

revelation and the answers to the great religious problems of existence *outside the course of history*. People moved in the eternal circle of the cosmos which, strictly speaking, has no purpose but revolves eternally within itself. The mythological view of time is *cyclical*. The problems of life and death, or generation and decay, fertility and destruction, return generation after generation, but are 'eternal', i.e. they are in all times and in all places fundamentally the same. What happens in the world (historical factuality) is certainly a revelation of these eternal problems, it brings them to light, but has no effect on them. The history of people and countries forms, as it were, the scene on which the eternal realities appear before the footlights and become visible, but this history neither adds nor subtracts anything essential to or from this reality. The real, the metaphysical, the religious is in essence without time or place and cannot be influenced by historical events. It is for this reason that we say that in polytheistic mythological thought there is no room for something like history in the real sense of the word.

The same is true of the *revelation of the divine*. There is a 'divine order' which opens itself in the world and reveals itself and the deepest dimension of reality. This revelation consists in people becoming aware, through the events of life, of the supra-temporal, even the a-temporal, dimension of so many realities which transcend them, and in their being opened to, in their becoming conscious of, the transparency of *the cosmic events themselves as the one, eternal divine reality*, in which they together with all other beings are subsumed. The religious reveals itself not in non-repeatable and contingent historical events,[2] but in that which throughout all these events continually remains the same: the great natural phenomena, the 'borderline situations' with which people are confronted (suffering, death, generation, reproduction, fertility, sickness, disaster, wars, joy and ecstasy, unexplainable phenomena, etc.). These mythological religions are fundamentally *natural religions*. The superhuman order, the real religious reality which in the end the universe is, the great sacred reality of which everything is in one way or another a part, reveals itself in the 'eternal', superhuman, continually returning phenomena which cannot essentially be touched by history. What exists is an eternal cosmic cycle whose holy, divine character manifests itself to humanity. History, as we already said, plays here, as history, no role at all. Nothing really occurs in history. Human generations succeed one another endlessly – and in this sense one can speak of history – but the only thing that happens is that every human generation stands again before the same metaphysical problems in which the eternal, unhistorical, non-evolving but cyclically returning essence of the holy becomes transparent. Every phase of the world event has, religiously speaking, the same meaning. It is a monument of the 'hierophany' (= sacred self-manifestation) of the eternally divine cosmic reality. Nothing is non-repeatable. No single historical event subtracts from or adds to the essential. For this reason history in the course of its contingent events is no place where God can be found. Nature and the 'eternal' characteristics of people and the world are the places.

In such a world view it makes no sense to say that history *is going somewhere;* just as it makes no sense to say that there is a certain line or evolution in history, or that one could draw a line in it. The express religious qualities within the pagan mythological world view are resignation and the maintenance of the existing order. The great religious concern of the pagan is safety before the powers which can always threaten his existence. Cult and magic must serve to guarantee this safety before the gods. Religion has nothing to do with an historical project but everything to do with maintaining a good relationship with the gods who personify and represent the great cosmic powers and who must guarantee the 'good order'.

As was said, the image of time is a cycle and in such a view one *cannot speak of hope.* Indeed, hope in what? Since the world is going nowhere... World events have no real goal. The eternal cycle of the self-manifestation of the divine is literally without a goal! One cannot say within the mythological world that history as history can reveal something of the divine. All events and all historical figures continually reveal the same, namely, that the divine reality exists and events and figures are all essentially the same.

This is well illustrated by the annals or the images of the

Egyptian pharaohs and the kings of Mesopotamia. All these rulers are in the end nothing other than links in the permanent hierophany of the divine order in the human community. They lack, as it were, historical individuality. Their own particular reason for existing consists in being a sort of 'incarnation' of the divine order. The king is a revelation of the ultimate divine character of authority and order and coincides with it. In the well known Akkadian 'myth of Etanna' we read that 'the monarchy descended from heaven'. The pharaoh was considered the son of the sun god Re, even his incarnation; after his death he was subsumed into the pantheon of the gods. The monarchy is indeed an exemplary sacral reality. The king is the sacred link between the people of his country and the divine world. He is a sort of living rite, a 'sacrament of the divine order'. From king to king, the divine order preserves itself as a guarantee of the stability of human society. Even though the mythology of the king in Egypt is not exactly the same as in Akkad, Assyria or Babylon, the divine function of the ruler is still present.

The cyclical mythological world view is thus free of all history. It is a timeless present. No single historical moment is privileged as a 'moment of revelation' above any other; no single historical fact is essential nor is any single fact non-repeatable (nothing new under the sun!). *The divine reveals itself universally*, above time and space; divine revelation is never tied to a particular fact, a particular period, people, land or person. Put in philosophical terms, divine revelation (meaning revelation of the religious character of reality) is not tied to contingent historical factuality. The great myths of the ancient peoples reflect this view very well, the mythical events occur outside time and space or, what amounts to the same, they take place *always and everywhere*.[3] The revelation of the divine is the same over the whole world and for all time. *The question of the meaning of history as history therefore has no home in mythological thought.*

Surprisingly enough the Bible itself contains an unsurpassed example of the cyclical view of time in the famous book Ecclesiastes (Qoheleth), the book from the third century before Christ written under the motto, 'vanity of vanities, and all is vanity'. This book is also the source of our expression, 'there is nothing new under the sun! We offer a quotation which reflects Qoheleth's view of time,

> A generation goes, and a generation comes, but the earth remains for ever. The sun rises and the sun goes down, and hastens to the place where it rises. The wind blows to the south, and goes round to the north; round and round goes the wind, and on its circuits the wind returns. All streams run to the sea, but the sea is not full; to the place where the streams flow, there they flow again. All things are full of weariness; a man cannot utter it, the eye is not satisfied with seeing, nor the ear with hearing. What has been is what will be, and what has been done is what will be done; and there is nothing new under the sun. Is there a thing of which it is said, "see, this is new"? It has been already, in the ages before us. There is no remembrance of former things, nor will there be remembrance of later things yet to happen among those who come after (Eccles 1:4-11).

It is no accident that Qoheleth meditates on the absolute lack of meaning of what happens under the sun, all is vanity and a striving after wind. This book, which has an exceptional place in the Bible in terms of its view of life, is also unique in terms of its conception of time.

The biblical world view tells us that not nature but history is the place where God is revealed

The world view developed in Israel differs fundamentally from the mythological world view. Many are of the opinion that Israel (meaning the biblical culture) is the birthplace of real historical consciousness. In any case, for so far as is known the Bible contains the oldest specific historiographic (i.e. non-mythological) texts in all of world literature (namely, the stories around the succession to David's throne, 2 Sam 9-20 and 1 Kings 1-2, five centuries before Herodotus). Of course, we can apply to

33

Israel's historical consciousness the saying 'Rome was not built in a day'. Breaking free from the mythological world view was naturally a slow (and a never – at least in biblical times – completed) process.[4] In the Bible there are still many traces of mythological thinking and mythological representations, which also in Israel formed the fertile ground of religious language and cult. Nevertheless, historical thinking is something distinctive, and a wholly unique characteristic of the biblical view of God and his revelation. For methodological reasons we will limit ourselves in our presentation to that distinction, and will leave the other elements (to be precise, everything in which Israel was closely related with the surrounding religions) out of the discussion.

Israel's historical consciousness is of cardinal importance for the view of what revelation can be. Israel worked itself free of the mythological world view by *radically removing the cosmos from the realm of the sacred* and by thinking of God as *transcending* the world. God fulfils *no function* within the universe. He is not even a part of it. In this way the notion of 'creation' enters history; the world is experienced as non-divine. In this sense the Bible is the most secularizing and profane book one could imagine. For the Bible the world is radically world, not divine, but 'merely' God's creation. For this reason, in Israel the concept 'revelation' will no longer be the self-manifestation of the divine character of the universe in events, nature, gods and people, but rather an authentic *relationship* between God and a world which must be radically separated from God's essence and to which God, as not deducible from the world, reveals himself in a free act.

In this reversal with regard to the universe, in the desacralization of the universe, possibilities are created for thinking in terms of an historical revelation, or better, *revelation as history*. In Israel time has broken out of its pointless cycle and has become *linear*. We become able to think of history as *going somewhere*, as having a goal. (Seen purely philosophically this latter can be questioned; we represent here only the Bible's own point of view.) We see also the arrival of one of the most fundamental notions which has come to determine biblical faith, *hope*. There is hope for history! Another very important result of this linear conception of time is that people are no longer called to undergo the cycle of eternal destiny taking place over their heads, but rather are themselves called to play a role in history, they *will make history*. This implies that mankind *becomes responsible for history!* Events and people are no longer a continuous repetition of the same. They no longer all have the same unalterable meaning, but play an individual role in world events not subject to replacement or substitution. There can be moments of progress, but also of regression with regard to the hope to which history is called. (The object of the final hope will be expressed in Israel with the term 'the kingdom of God'.) In other words, people can play both a positive and a negative role in history.[5]

An illustration of this can be found in the Bible's fundamentally different view of kingship when compared to that of Egypt or Babylon. The Bible has secularized its kings! It calls its kings before the tribunal of history – actually of God's judgement over history – and condemns many of its rulers as bad. Such a thing is not possible in a world view where human history is itself the divine, nor in a view where the king is the manifestation of the divine. In Israel the king is the highest servant of God, rules in God's name, is even 'son of God' – but in the Bible this is by no means a reason simply to identify the king's will with God's will. The king must listen to God's word and obey it, he does not coincide with it! In Israel the kings are servants of Yahweh, but they are no 'hierophany', no manifestation of the divine. They can err, and God can reject them, something which, for example, is unthinkable for a pharaoh in Egypt's classical period because the pharaoh is himself divine, the incarnation of the divine character of the social order. His standpoint is then obviously the correct one, it coincides with and is the expression of the will of the gods. But in the biblical view no individual person can identify himself in this way with God.[6]

All this has had an enormous influence on the concept 'revelation'. According to the biblical view, God's self-revelation takes place in *what people experience and do*. There are people

35

and historical events which can obscure God, there are those which help in discovering him. Put differently, *what humanity knows about God is no longer independent of what happened in history.* In Israel the idea could develop that certain non-repeatable events, certain non-repeatable persons could be places where God could be found; that this is even the case for the unexchangeable and non-repeatable history of a particular people in a given period of history. The non-repeatable, un-exchangeable, non-deducible and fortuitous (= not necessary) reality is referred to in theology and philosophy as the contingent reality (ref. note 9). In Israel there developed an experience of history as contingent reality and, what is fundamental for biblical belief in revelation, an experience of *the contingent reality as a place where God can be found.* Put differently, the Bible believes that God allows himself to be found and known (that he 'reveals' himself) in the *active responsible history of humanity.* The religion of Israel is *no longer a natural religion.* The first and central point of faith for Israel is not that 'God is the one who reveals himself in nature' but that 'God is the one who brought us out of Egypt'! Israel 'read' its God in historical events, not primarily in nature or the 'eternal or unchanging' aspects of life. This is also the meaning of expressions such as, 'Yahweh is the God of Abraham, Isaac and Jacob. Yahweh is the God of Moses.' And later, 'God is the God of Jesus Christ.' Exegetes have long known that the biblical texts whose express theme is 'creation theology' (e.g. Josh 40; Gen 1; Ps 104) are all more recent than the texts which speak of saving the people of Israel and the covenant with God. Creation theology in Israel is much younger than 'historical theology' and, what is more, biblical creation theology was developed completely within the framework and *in function of* the historical revelation of God. For the Bible, creation and nature form, as it were, the 'decor' against which God's saving activity in history takes place.

Christians, together with their Jewish brothers, believe that this notion of revelation originates with God himself – but even when one does not share this belief, it is easy to understand what a 'revolution' such a view as this had brought about in the world and how revolutionary it still is. Very many people can even now only accept the mythological image of revelation which says that God (generally seen as 'the' divine) reveals himself outside of time and place, i.e. free of concrete and contingent historical figures or events, everywhere and always universally in the same way, namely, in confrontation of 'eternal man' with 'eternal problems'. The historical image of God's revelation, namely, that certain unexchangeable and non-repeatable events and people can be the place where God can be found, remains in our time a major stumbling block for many and often the main reason why they reject the Christian biblical faith. It cannot be denied that the concept of an *historical revelation* (which also implies being bound to *relative* facts and events) is the greatest exasperation and 'weakness' of biblical faith for human reason. This is the reason why many people – even believers! – prefer to continue speaking of God in the context of nature and human borderline situations (birth and death, for example) rather than in the context of history. Yet the concept of historical revelation is the *sine qua non* for accepting the unique position of Jesus of Nazareth in revelation. The concept of historical revelation is the *Bible's absolutely unique contribution to world history*.

It is evident that numerous consequences flow from this. People are no longer invited to look for God outside of or above history but in the heart of historical contingency. History itself, with all its searching and failing, with all the relativity of historical situations and with humanity's responsibility in them, is the place where people can learn who God could really be. Not unhistorical nature, thought to be unchangeable, but human history is the best way to faith. From this is derived the core concept of the Bible, *God is a God of people*.

Another extremely important characteristic is that one can say of mythological faith in nature that 'it requires no commitment'. In other words, natural religion is not in essence ethical.[7] The ethical behaviour of pious pagans has no influence on the efficacy – for, this is the heart of the matter – of the sacrifices performed, for example, in honour of a fertility god. A sacrifice is essentially functional as is the whole religion. Pagan religion's goal has nothing to do with any special relationship to the deity. Put simply, so long as I bring Baal the sacrifices due for the fertility of my family and my fields, Baal could not care less whether or not I persecute my neighbour. For the pagan mythological religions, morality is an essential element of order in the cosmos, and there is always a god to look after morality, but morality does not, as such, determine the quality of the relationship between God and his people. In the Bible it is very different. There the prophets have God say that he is disgusted by the sacrifices brought by hypocrites or by people who are unjust to their fellows. The value of the sacrifice is no longer 'magically functional' but is completely subservient to the moral quality of human life. (See, for example, texts such as Is 1:10-20; 58:1-12; Amos 2:6-8; 4:1-5; 5:21-27.) A sacrifice (or more broadly, a rite, a liturgical act) is only meaningful within the framework of and as expression of a particular quality of life. With the inclusion of human responsibility for history within the search for God, an intrinsic and permanent bond is created in the Bible between the ethical quality of human life and the relationship to God. Here lies the ultimate reason why the Bible will be able to say that the most important places where God can be found, the places where God most deeply reveals himself, are *love* and *justice*. Humanity's ultimate responsibility before history is to create love and justice. When Paul later says, 'for he who loves his neighbour has fulfilled the law' (Rom 13:8), and when John says, 'He who does not love, does not know God; for God is love' (1 Jn 4:8), we have reached the most extreme consequences of the biblical view of revelation. When the heart of Jesus' message is – and in our opinion, it is so – 'Love one another, for God loves you' (see the sermon on the mount), then he has indeed, as Matthew writes, 'fulfilled the Law'. Love and justice, which can only be realized by people in historical activity, are for the Bible the real places where God can be found. These two are realized only where people liberate one another. Love and freedom are correlative concepts; the one is not possible without the other. That is why the Bible detects God everywhere where a liberating act is performed. Put differently, the Bible reads God's will in liberating activity. It cannot, therefore, be merely by chance that the theme at the heart of every belief and hope and of every representation of God in the Scriptures always revolves around liberation. Yahweh is essentially *the one who freed Israel from bondage*. Jesus is essentially *the Redeemer*, i.e. the one who radically frees humanity from all slavery be it the slavery of injustice and egoism, of sin and evil, up to and including the ultimate slavery of subjugation to death. Confessing Jesus the redeemer means we believe that God's liberating love does not have to surrender to death. The liberation of Israel, commemorated in the passover, is completed in Christ's Easter. This thought determines the structure of the Christian faith.

It has by now become clear just how much the New Testament's view of history is a child of the Old's. What we wrote at the beginning of this chapter can now be repeated: history is something essential for the gospels. Because God reveals himself in *concrete* history and because the highest revelation of God is linked to Jesus (Jesus is 'The Word of God'), *Jesus' real history* is of fundamental importance for understanding the gospel's message. Jesus is confessed as the Messiah, as the Son of God, *because of the concrete manner in which he lived, because of what he said and did, because of what happened to him in Jerusalem*. Not a mythological figure, nor a personified idea but a concrete living person is important for the Christian faith. This is the reason why the Church has always rejected esoteric, gnostic and docetic representations of Christ.[8] Lest Jesus' divine sonship be mythological, it *demands* his radical, concrete and contingent humanity and history. If Jesus, for example, did not really die, his death would have no meaning for anyone!

In the light of the preceding, it is evident that there is a fundamental difference between the assertion, 'History is essential for the Bible' and the assertion, 'Everything mentioned in the Bible really happened historically'. Just this difference (or rather, not seeing this difference) has led to numerous misunderstandings, many of which have not yet been eliminated. We cannot sufficiently emphasize that the ancient biblical authors did not write history according to the norms for modern scientific research, nor did they intend to do this. Just as Titus Livy attributes speeches to Hannibal which this Carthaginian general never uttered, but which serve to make clear for the reader the significance of events when interpreting Livy, so too with the biblical authors. The fact that a biblical person approaches the world 'historically' and not 'mythologically' means something completely different from saying that everything in the Bible is exact according to scientifically historical norms. Measured by *those* norms, the Bible is anything but historical, and *this is also true for certain pages of the New Testament!* A simple example can clarify the difference. When a student of modern history asserts that pharaoh Ramses II was knocked out in the third round by Nigel Mansell during the Olympic Games held in New York in 1302, then he has made a scientifically historical error. This, however, does not mean that the student thinks mythologically, he thinks of the world in historical terms. It is his facts that are wrong. Of course, one cannot push this distinction to the absurd in the sense that one could say that the historical Jesus is of fundamental importance for the faith even if all that the evangelists say about him is total nonsense. There would be no historical Jesus left. But on that point we can rest easy. The basic historical information which we possess about Jesus is clear enough to ground the specific characteristics of the Christian faith! E.P. Sanders correctly writes, '... We can know rather well what Jesus wanted to accomplish, we can know rather a lot about what he said, and we can also know that both these things took place within the Jewish world of the first century.'[9]

In the following section we will have a closer look at the biblical view of the relationship between revelation and human history. We will apply the biblical view of historical revelation to a question which is very important for the gospel, i.e. what is the relationship between Jesus' history and faith? Put differently, what does Jesus tell us about God? How is Jesus the pre-eminent place for finding God, how is he the self-revelation of God? How can *his* word be called *Word of God*? Or again, how do the gospels themselves interpret Jesus as revelation of God?

The history of Jesus as a symbol of God

To summarize briefly, for the Bible, history is the place where God becomes known (or better, where he reveals himself). Conversely, without history God is not revealed. The human history is thus the 'medium' through which God becomes a knowable communicable reality. In other words, for humanity history is the *symbol of God*. The term *symbol* requires, in our context, some explanation. One of the ways in which modern theology tries to approach the relationship between God and the world is the way which the Germans call *Realsymbolik* where the symbol is no longer thought of as something opposite to reality but the only means by which a certain reality (especially 'spiritual' realities) attain a knowable existence; *Realsymbolik* has become an important element of present day explanation of sacramental reality.

We found an interesting and illuminating approach to the theme 'history as symbol' as it relates to the New Testament in an article by the American exegete Sandra Schneiders on the Gospel of John.[10] What she writes about John is equally applicable to all the gospels. They all write history as symbol. We incorporate Schneiders' vision in the following explanation.

Schneiders tries to find a good definition for symbol using the now classic distinction between symbol and sign. She writes:

> There is growing consensus among scholars concerned with language in general and religious language in particular that symbol and sign are not equivalent terms. A sign is something which stands for an absent reality. Its task is to refer the observer to something other than itself. A billboard, for example, is a sign. A symbol, on the contrary, is the sensible expression of a present reality. Its task is to make the transcendent, or some aspect of the Transcendent, intersubjectively available and to mediate the participation of the observer in that which it reveals. The human body is the primary symbol of the personality. Speech is a symbol of inner experience. Art symbolizes the beautiful. The Church is the symbol of

41

Christ. Most importantly, Jesus is the symbol of God. In short, a symbol never stands for something. It is the sensible expression of the transcendent, that is, it is the *locus* of revelation (human or divine) and of participation in that which is revealed.

To clarify, Schneiders means that the symbolized reality is not 'absent' from the symbol, i.e. it does not exist 'apart from' the symbol, or it does not, in any case, assume a knowable and communicable shape apart from what symbolizes it. The symbol is the event (thing, word, signal,...) that makes the transcendent reality observable, intersubjectively available – transcendent reality which *at the same time both surpasses the symbol and cannot be known or seen without the symbol,* simply because it is transcendent (surpassing). In this way we understand the examples offered. The body is symbol of the person. The reality 'person' surpasses the body and is thus a transcendent reality but it cannot be seen, known or even realized apart from the body as its symbol. Similarly, language is a symbol of inner experience, even more, of thought itself, while art symbolizes beauty. Another good example is love. Love between people is nowhere coextensive with the symbols in which it is expressed. Love is a reality which transcends its symbols. Every symbol of love can also radically express lack of love. Whether it is a kiss, a look or a caress, sexual union, a smile, a present, a word... they are all expressions of love which can also be used to express the opposite. None of these expressions is the love itself. But all these expressions are real symbols of love in the sense that love, as transcendent reality, can only be made intersubjectively known and available in symbols. Although love surpasses its symbols, it does not really 'exist' without symbols. Just as the human person really does not 'exist' without his body as symbol, as thought does not exist without language or beauty without the numerous symbols in which it is expressed (art, music, etc.). Within this linguistic play, a symbol could be described as *a reality which gives shape to a transcendental reality which is distinctive from it but which can only exist in it.*

A few supplementary examples can clarify further the distinction between symbol and sign.

There is an important point which should be remembered in examining these examples. A symbol is always at the same time something else than a symbol. It is also 'unsymbolically itself'. A Rolls-Royce can be a status symbol, but it is first and foremost 'unsymbolically' an object, namely, a car. A kiss can be a symbol of love, but it is first and foremost a physical contact of lips; language is a symbol of thought, but it is at the same time a body of phonetic elements tied to a particular structure. It must be posited that if the symbols were not also something other than symbol, namely, observable phenomena free of their symbolic reference, then they could not be symbols at all. The reality symbolized (e.g. love) does not exist as a knowable and communicable reality apart from the symbol, but the symbol (e.g. the kiss) has its own existence independent of what it symbolizes. Put differently, water does not cease being water (H_2O) because it is the symbol of purity; oil does not cease being oil because it is the symbol of kingship. It can really not be said that water is either real or symbolic; the body is either real or symbolic. All these things can only be symbols to the extent that they are also themselves as 'naked' reality. A symbol is therefore never a bynecessity and of itself a symbol. It is *never a symbol free of all interpretation*! A symbol can always be looked upon and 'read' as non-symbolic. A ring can be read as a symbol of faithfulness (an in a certain context, e.g. a marriage ceremony, it is spontaneously so read), but this is not necessary in and of itself. The ring can always be read as what it primarily is, a circular shaped sliver of gold.

Because symbols are not themselves the symbolized reality, but lead an existence of their own, they only become symbol by virtue of the interpretation they receive from a given context. This implies that symbols can shift. No limits can be put to this shifting, theoretically *anything can be a symbol of anything*. That is why the *frame of reference* is of such enormous importance for understanding a symbol. When the frame of reference in which a symbol functions is not known, or when it is misinterpreted, the symbol can easily be misunderstood, or understood not at all. This is why symbols are generally and spontaneously understood in a given period (and therefore never need to be explicitly explained, e.g. a handshake or a dove with an olive branch), and are not at all understood in another period. This explains why biblical or liturgical symbols which were everyday matters centuries ago are no longer understood by the present generation. On the other hand, new symbols are growing among the young which the older generations do not understand. The frame of reference again is of fundamental importance for the functioning of symbols. In a marriage the ring is a symbol of love and faithfulness, but in Tolkien's trilogy *The Lord of the Rings* the ring is the symbol of the enslaving power of evil. On a socialist poster the rose has another symbolic value than in Umberto Eco's book *The Name of the Rose*, and the whiteness of Moby Dick in Herman Melvill's book of that name on a demonic whale cannot be taken for a symbol of purity or innocent joy.

A good example of the importance of the frame of reference for understanding symbolism can be found in the story of the exorcism in the land of the Gerasenes, Mk 5:1-20 (par. Mt 8:28-34; Lk 8:26-39. Note meanwhile the differences in detail: Gerasenes versus Gadarenes; 2 possessed in Mt versus 1 in Mk and Lk). Various elements are interwoven in this story such as the (historical) recollection of the exorcisms performed by Jesus; folk legends about the herd of pigs, which make the whole into a rather spectacular miracle; but above all the symbolic or catechetical meaning of the story in the gospel. The story – when read in depth – wants to say that Jesus also came for the gentiles, that he also wants to withdraw the gentiles from the power of evil (the devil) rather than leave them in its power – as many expected that the Messiah would do. But to understand this one has to understand the frame of reference of the story. Pigs – the pre-eminent example of forbidden animals – are for Jewish believers *the* symbol of the gentiles' impurity and lawlessness. When it is known that Jesus' miracle took place on the other side of the sea, i.e. in the so-called 'Decapolis', which was gentile territory, then the symbolic meaning becomes clear. Jesus conquers the impurity of the gentiles and hurls it into the depths of the sea. This symbolism corresponds to the recollection preserved of the historical Jesus, for christendom did indeed open the door to bringing the Good News to the gentiles, in the full belief that it was being faithful to Jesus' own deepest intentions. Whoever no longer understands the frame of reference of this symbol can only see in this miracle story an unintelligible and even offensive (Is Jesus not being unjust to the owners of the herd of pigs?) story, which is more of a stumbling stone for faith rather than a guide toward it!

From here we can return to history. In principle, we cannot posit the alternative: either history or symbol. If history is not first of all un-symbolically itself – i.e. contingent, 'real' historical facts – it is unable to be a symbol. On the other hand it is equally true that history as naked factuality is never able to say or reveal anything. This is only possible when it is read as a symbol – when it is interpreted! A ring does not mean anything so long as it is read as only a bent fragment of metal. With regard to history Sandra Schneiders writes,

> The most characteristic specific difference of the Judeo-Christian tradition is its conviction that God revealed himself and was encountered in history. History, in other words, is symbolic within this tradition… In the Fourth Gospel, however, the notion of symbolic revelation becomes fully explicit. The Johannine concentration of all revelation and all response to revelation in the person of Jesus of Nazareth whom he designates as the Word *become* flesh (1:14), that is, as the symbolization of God, is the clearest indication of this fact and the principle of all its consequences.

What Schneiders says of John's gospel is equally applicable to all the gospels, even to the whole of Scripture. Thus an evangelist does, indeed, want to write real history, but history as symbol of God's reality. God's reality is expressed in the world in no other way than *in and through history as its symbol*. In this sense a gospel is symbolic from its first letter to its last. It wants above all to express that the history of Jesus of Nazareth, as real history, is one and all symbol of God's reality. Jesus is, in his earthly and human reality, fundamentally the revelation – the Word! – of God. Jesus is the self-communication of God. Given this view, we understand the exceptional bearing of the dialogue with Philip in Jn 14:8ff, 'Philip said to him, "Lord, show us the Father, and we shall be satisfied." Jesus said to him, "Have I not been with you so long, and yet you do not know me, Philip? *He who has seen me has seen the Father; how can you say 'Show us the Father'?".'* Although Jesus is certainly not himself the Father and does not see himself as such, he says that there is no other entrance to the Father than through him. Every comparison is inadequate, but using the terminology about symbol seen above we could say, the Father, as it were, does not 'exist' (at least not 'for us') without Jesus. Here lies the ultimate foundation for later dogmatic pronouncements on Jesus' divinity and the impulse for the theology of the Trinity.[11]

In sum, a gospel can really only be a symbol *to the extent that* Jesus was a real and historical human reality. In this way, for example, Jesus' passion can only be a symbol of God's saving and liberating love for his people to the extent that his passion was real and historical. Historical reality is a symbol for God only *as* historical reality. It is for this reason that Jesus' real humanity is so important. Jesus can only be a symbol of God *by being a real person.* Remove the concrete historical reality from the person Jesus, and you return to mythology.

This ties in with what was said earlier,[12] namely, the gospels write *highly inspired* history. The gospels are written from the point of view which says, 'This is how we understand Jesus; this is for us the meaning of Jesus, in him we have seen Emmanuel, God with us.' The believing interpretation of Jesus' life is, in our opinion, well-founded and we subscribe to it, but this does not diminish the fact that the gospel, as the result of a believing interpretation, is an interpretation which needs the whole frame of reference of Israel's and Jesus' history if it to be understood in its true scope. In principle, one *can* always read the history of Jesus as not being a symbol of God, because this history is in the first place what it is, namely, a body of events, situations, words, etc. related to the figure of Jesus. In other words, a believing reading of the gospel is *never absolutely compulsory* – that Jesus is the Son of God cannot be proven as one proves that a triangle has 180 degrees or that the earth is round! That Jesus is the real and definitive (*eschatological*) self-expression of God in this world can only be read within the frame of reference of the total reality of faith. Reading the gospel from an atheistic or psychological starting point or from an interest in the history of religion still remains possible. Even the frame of reference of the critical biblical sciences (text criticism, literary criticism or historical criticism) does not take into consideration this symbolic dimension of Jesus' history; it is not even able to disclose it. One does not come to believe in Jesus because of good textual criticism or good exegesis, however necessary of useful these may be!

There is one more point to be made in this chapter. When the gospels intend to describe the authentic history of Jesus, they are not concerned with offering an exact reconstruction as an external 'proof' that he was the Messiah, but rather with offering a believing interpretation whose cornerstone is the Easter experience (the resurrection). In other words, the gospels offer an *in-depth reading* of the events around Jesus. All the stories in the gospel are directly intended to express the religious dimension (or better, the significance for the faith) of Jesus' history, to express the symbolic dimension of his person and mission. Every story wants to express the 'transparency' of Jesus' story as it relates to God. A gospel can be compared with a portrait painted by a great artist. A real artist will not only – and not even in the first place – try to make his portrait 'real', but will allow the in-depth dimension of the subject to become apparent. Schneiders writes quite correctly,

To ask how the Johannine account corresponds to what 'actually happened' is like asking how Van Gogh's self-portrait corresponds to his historical face. The question is misplaced. The significant question is how does the self-portrait of Van Gogh correspond to the person of Van Gogh. Any amateur on Monmartre could have copied Van Gogh's face. Only the artist could create a new symbolic expression of his person.

Applied to Christ in the gospels this means that the correct question is not whether the portrait of Christ in the gospels agrees with his historical appearance, but whether it agrees with the reality of his person. What Schneiders says so well of John's gospel holds equally true for every gospel, a gospel is a *literary icon of Christ.*

A very important aspect is related to this. It is possible to write stories whose events did not really take place, but which express the meaning of what did take place! Put differently, the symbolic dimension of Jesus' life story can, as it were, *exist independently as story*. In this case we have 'purely' symbolic stories, but they are meaningless without the real history of Jesus whose in-depth dimension they express. There is no doubt that such stories are present in the gospel. John has gone farthest in including them, but the other gospels also contain such (often old, traditional) stories.

Three clear examples:
– The descent of the Holy Spirit in the shape of a dove on Jesus at his baptism (cf Mt 3:16f; Mk 1:10f; Lk 3:21f; Jn 1:33f. Note well the 'discrepancies' in agreement among the four versions.) It is really not necessary to believe that the Holy Spirit descended in the form of a dove to grasp the full meaning of the story. Jesus' baptism (which 'really happened') becomes, in the Christian tradition, Jesus' 'investiture' by the Father for the mission which will now begin. The descent of the Spirit reveals the symbolic dimension of the otherwise unremarkable fact of Jesus' baptism amid the mass of other people whom John baptized.
– Jesus walks on the sea (Mt 14:25ff; Mk 6:48ff; Jn 6:16ff). Such a story shows, among other things, that Jesus (as risen Lord) dominates the forces of Evil which cause storm and head-wind in life. Of course, this symbolic story becomes meaning-less if it is not supported by the real story of Jesus' life and death! This and the previous example also illustrate that the Bible reader's concern must not be to know what happened exactly, but rather, to try to understand what the *text* wants to say. Han Renckens is correct in writing, 'What we have to

explain is the text, not the events behind the text; the main concern is not Bible History, but the Bible.'[13] $\mathcal{M}$

– The third example does not involve a particular text, but a general procedure followed by the evangelists. Very often we find in the gospels, at a given event or in the words spoken by Jesus or others, a reference to a text in the Old Testament. When the reference is explicit (there are also very many implicit references) the evangelist adds a declaration something like 'this happened to fulfil the words of the prophet... who said...'. Matthew, especially, does this frequently. But when we read the biblical quotations in their original context, we note that in general they do not at all relate to the situation in the gospel where the quotation is used. The impression is often given that the scriptural texts are dragged in to force the events around Jesus to agree with the Scriptures. This is clearly the case in the infancy narrative in Matthew. In Mt 2:15, in the context of the flight to Egypt, Hos 11:1 is cited, 'Out of Egypt I have called my son.' The original text does not at all refer to the child Jesus, but to the liberation of Israel from Egypt. In Mt 2:18, as commentary on the infanticide in Bethlehem, the prophet Jeremiah is cited (31:15), 'A voice was heard in Ramah, wailing and loud lamentation, Rachel weeping for her children; she refused to be consoled, because they were no more.' Originally, this text refers to a fictive lamentation of the tribal mother of the Israelites over their misery and exile after the fall of Samaria. The very fact that Matthew transplants citations from their original context to a new context shows us where the intention of these quotations lies. Standing within the tradition of biblical salvation history and hope, the evangelists use the texts of God's time-honoured revelation to disclose the deep symbolic dimension of events and words around Jesus. By saying that Hosea's prophesy is fulfilled in Jesus' flight to Egypt, Matthew shows that Jesus in his personal history represents and recapitulates the whole history of his people (bondage in and liberation from Egypt). What happened to Israel at the exodus will receive its fulfilment in Jesus. Relating the infanticide to Israel's destruction and exile similarly is intended to illustrate Jesus salvation historical dimension. Matthew says that what happened to

49

Jesus happened 'from God' and has its (fulfilling!) place in the salvation history of the people of Israel.

≥ An interesting assignment relating to this second chapter, which can be done individually or in a group, is to look up the original context of a number of the evangelists' scriptural citations in the Bible and then try to understand what symbolic dimension the citation in its new context confers on the events and words around Jesus. By way of suggestion we mention: Mt 1:23; 3:3; 4:15-16; 5:4-5; 8:17; 9:13 (cp 12:7); 11:5; 11:10; 12:18-21; 13:13-15; 15:8-9; 18:40; 21:5; 21:16; 22:37-39; 26:15; 27:9-10; Mk 11:15-17; 12:1,10-11; 15:34,36; Lk 4:18-19; Jn 2:17; 6:31; 13:18; 19:24,28,36-37. ≤

NOTES

1   The term 'polytheistic' means characterized by the worship of many gods. The collection of the various divinities of a polytheistic religion is called a 'pantheon'. The term 'mythological' is, of course, derived from 'myth' (Greek *muthos*). By 'myths' we mean the old stories which take place in the world of the gods in a primaeval period. In the context of our presentation it is above all important to know that the old myths functioned as stories used to explain the great realities and problems of existence: death and life, natural phenomena, fertility, etc. Since every aspect of existence can raise questions as to the why of things, innumerable mythological stories grew. The myth tries to answer the great mysterious 'why' of existence. The myth's answer is unscientific and pre-philosophical, and is essentially religious. The myth is often closely related to cult (liturgy) in which ancient man ritually celebrated the (religious) mystery of existence. The myth accompanies the rituals as an explanatory story.

2   The basic meaning of the word 'contingent' is 'arbitrary, accidental, that which exists or occurs without necessarily having to exist or occur'. Contingent (contingency) is an extremely important concept in philosophy and theology. Applied to historical events we use the word with the meaning that events are contingent in so far as they are neither necessary, nor general, nor constant nor as such repeatable. Concretely we refer to all historical events seen from the point of view of their factuality. Every historical fact is, however we turn it, *this* fact and no other. When a given event or act is repeated its contingency is not abrogated, the first event and the repetition are both contingent historical events. Thus, for example, the Second World War, the coronation of a king, or the baking of a loaf of bread are contingent historical events, in the sense that they are non-repeatably *these* facts and no other, and that they are neither necessary nor general.

3   We find a classic example of this in the magnificent Greek myth of Demeter

and Persephone which was told in Eleusis during the cultic celebration of the autumnal sowing. Demeter, the mother goddess of the fertile earth and of grain, has a daughter, Persephone, who is abducted by the god of the underworld, Hades (Pluto). After many vicissitudes, Hades is compelled by his brother, the supreme god Zeus, to return Persephone to her mother. However, during one third of the year she returns to Hades in the underworld. This mythological story celebrated the sacred mystery of the grain that is sown and grows to be harvested. Persephone personifies the seed that is hidden from June until October in the storage rooms of the underworld, but when sown again joins the earth (Persephone's mother) where it remains until the harvest. This myth is told as something that once happened in some former time, but is in fact intended to celebrate and explain an aspect of the eternally returning sacred mystery of fertility.

4   There is an important remark to be added here. We are aware that we have used the terms 'myth' and 'mythology' in a specific context of the history of culture. The important problem of whether 'mythical language' is and must remain a necessary vehicle of faith and religious expression cannot be treated within the confines of our discussion. This problem has to do with the relationship between historical revelation and natural theology, and is currently a burning issue. But let it be clear that when we make a distinction between the pagan mythological world view and Israel's 'historical' faith we do not intend to assert that Israel would have found no references to God in nature or in life's boarder situations, or that the Bible would no longer use mythic language in its later stages. Israel would not have been able to read history as the place where God is found, if there was nowhere a contact point between historical experience and the 'natural' religiosity which Israel shared with the pagan religions. This latter also holds true for us today.

5   The opposition between 'cyclical' and 'linear' is portrayed severely black and white in this exposition for reasons of clarity. Reality is, of course, much 'more grey'. Neither in the Bible nor in pagan texts can this distinction be so finely drawn, even if it be only because Israel's linguistic arsenal and images are so closely related to that of the neighboring cultures. Here we try only offer in relief the decisive basic distinction as *global conception*. As to the rest, when we use the terms 'desacralization' and 'secularization' we do not intend to imply that the universe no longer has any association with the notion holy at all, but only that the cosmos does not have its holiness and venerability in and of itself. The cosmos can only be called holy to the degree that it is created and radically accepted by God. Creation is of itself not holy, not a part of the divinity, not a necessary emanation of it. If we can use the term holy with regard to the universe it refers only to a sanctity of a relational type. The cosmos (nature,...) is only holy to the degree God freely enters into a relationship with it.

6   Even the later concept of incarnation as applied to Jesus is no return to the mythological sacralization of a person! This is a theological misunderstanding which unfortunately dominated many centuries and which even now still lives in some of the representations made of Jesus. Speaking of Jesus as the 'Son of God' and also the concept of 'Christ's divinity' do indeed refer to an identification of Jesus' word with that of God, even of Jesus with God, but not in a mythological way. Jesus is not Yahweh in human form... As far as the kings

of Israel are concerned, many biblical texts still show signs of a royal mythology. But these are traces of influence from the surrounding pagan world view.

7 A clear distinction should be made here between natural religion and the modern problem of care for nature. Respect and care for nature can be an important historical and ethical task. The modern ecological question is an overwhelming illustration. However, this is quite different from what we mean here in our culture historical context. Yet, ecological care could also wander off in the direction of a renewed mythological sacralization of nature.

8 The terms 'docetic' and 'docetism' are derived from a Greek root which means 'appearance'. Docetic representations of Christ are, therefore, representations which accept the whole physical, contingent and historical humanity of Jesus, with all the limitations inherent to humanity only as appearance, or else rejects it completely. The so-called 'gnostic' tendencies which, as the word says, approach faith primarily as a body of hidden 'knowledge' and which are therefore often very 'esoteric' (i.e. for the initiated), generally promote docetic representations of Christ. The ecclesiastical rejection of docetism is an historical constant in theology. Nevertheless, the official condemnation has not hindered many popular, catechetical and devotional representation of Christ from remaining docetic.

9 E.P. Sanders, *Jesus and Judaism*. Philadelphia, 1985, p. 2. This problem is raised again further on in chapter 4.

10 S. Schneiders, 'History and Symbolism in the Fourth Gospel', in *L'Évangile de Jean* [*The Gospel of John*], ed. M. De Jong, BETL, XLIV, Leuven, University Press, 1977, p. 371-6.

11 To prevent any misunderstanding we should say that Jesus' answer to Philip may not lead to the conclusion that Jesus is the exclusive, sole symbol of God. If this were the case, the Old Testament would not be revelation. It would also mean that God could be detected or 'read' nowhere else than in Jesus. The expression 'who sees me, sees the Father' must be read positively and eschatologically, not exclusively. We must go even a step further. If, in the whole world, there was really no other symbol of God than Jesus, we would not be able to recognize that Jesus is a symbol of God.

12 See above, p. 23 .

13 H. Renckens, *De bijbel meemaken* [*Experiencing the Bible*], Kampen, 1988, p. 73.

3

A bird's-eye view
of the gospel tradition

In the following pages we will again take up the thread of chapter 1 and continue our search for the singular character of the gospels. To do this we will review the major milestones in the evolution leading to the development of the gospel literature.

Jesus of Nazareth

What we call 'the gospel tradition' begins, of course, with Jesus himself. *There* lies the gospel's firm historical basis. What Jesus of Nazareth said, how he lived, his relationship to people and the image of God he shaped there, his disputes with the authorities, his condemnation and death, the events which lie at the foundation of the faith in his resurrection, all these comprise the unexchangeable 'hard' core of the gospel literature. Because of their unbreakable bond with the historical Jesus, the gospels themselves are also really historical. In the previous chapter we examined the importance of history as philosophical and theological category. In the section on the symbolic dimension of history we discussed the importance of Jesus' own historicity with regard to the believing interpretation of his person as Word of God. There are still two important comments which we must add regarding the gospels' historicity.

Firstly, historicity, even as reflection of a correct recollection can be expressed by other means than via an exact account or a literal quotation. Historicity is wider than merely 'this is exactly the way it happened' or 'that is exactly what was said'. For example, according to a widely known tradition on 13 April, 1655, during the parliamentary session held in Paris, Louis XIV of France is to have spoken the words, *l'éat, c'est moi*. There is no doubt that this statement has been attributed to him falsely. Does that make it unhistorical? In the sense of a literal quotation, yes. But as a reflection of the Sun King's conception of the state, this utterance tersely touches the historical truth and expresses perfectly how King Louis pictured and experienced the relationship between state and sovereign. In other words, in the expression *l'état, c'est moi* an historical truth about Louis XIV is reported. But – and this is important! – this is not done free of all interpretation. If we can now say that this quotation conveys an historical truth, it is because Louis XIV has been 'put through' the interpretation of his contemporaries and of those who studied him after his death.

There is no doubt that we meet something similar in the gospels. They reflect the true historical shape of Jesus as he was experienced and 'read' by his disciples and contemporaries. They do this very often with words which are not cited literally, which were not written down while Jesus lived and which Jesus did not as such utter verbatim. It can be compared to the self-portrait by Van Gogh. The evangelists are not primarily concerned with painting a picture of Jesus which agrees with his face, but one which reveals in truth his person and which, from the point of view of a believing interpretation, sees in the history of Jesus the symbolic presence of God's saving reality. This is one of the elements which can help us understand why there is a difference between Matthew's version of the beatitudes and Luke's and why there are variants in the parables and miracle stories. Occasionally the interpretive reflection on Jesus goes very far, as in the noteworthy 'farewell discourse' in John's gospel. This so profound (and difficult) discourse (Jn 13-17) puts into words the intention and meaning of the passion – and of Jesus' whole mission – historically, i.e. fundamentally faithful to what Jesus really meant for the world, but there is no exegete who still considers it be a verbatim report of Jesus' words. Further on in our explanation it will become clear that this farewell discourse is, in a manner of speaking, in its entirety a brilliant creation of the fourth evangelist who brings to expression in it his theological view of Jesus Christ (his Christology). In essence, John, in his gospel, is doing exactly the same as what Paul does in his letters to the Galatians and Romans, namely, he is formulating his believing interpretation of the mystery of Christ. The 'perfidy' of the matter lies in the fact that John puts his theology in Jesus' words within the framework of his narrative about Jesus' life and death.

After two centuries experience in critically studying the gospel texts – a study carried out with a painful and sometimes unimaginable precision – exegesis had developed a good supply of safe 'tools for dissection' which allow them to recognize the literally exact reproduction of Jesus' own words (a verbatim quotation) on the one hand, and the interpreted reproduction, reworking and adaptation by tradition and even the creation of the evangelist on the other. For it is, of course, true that the gospels have passed down a considerable number of faithfully preserved, authentic sayings of Jesus. Oral transmission sometimes demonstrates tremendously strict accuracy – in that period when few people could write and no image media existed this was even stronger that is the case now – and the gospels contain often surprisingly untouched recollections of genuine facts about Jesus and above all words spoken by Jesus.

Secondly, the historical recollection of Jesus' words and deeds is thoroughly coloured by the *belief in his resurrection*. If it were not for this belief, there is a very good chance that we would never have heard of Jesus of Nazareth. For the disciples Jesus' resurrection was the experience through which they – at last! – understood Jesus' real meaning. In the resurrection, their 'eyes were opened'. From that position they, as it were, reread Jesus' entire appearance and saw everything in the light of their belief that God raised him from the dead and that he was indeed 'God's Anointed', i.e. the 'Christ' or the 'Messiah', the king and saviour of Israel. The French exegete D. Charpentier used a pleasing analogy for this believing reading:

To present a complicated diagram (an industrial drawing; the anatomy of the human body...) one uses occasionally the

55

technique of transparent plates, to the first, the basic drawing (e.g. the human skeleton), one or more drawings on transparent cellophane paper are added (e.g. muscles, circulatory system, organ...). In this way each drawing can be examined individually, but they can also be put on one another to provide an overview of the whole. About the same thing happened with the gospels. On the *fact of Jesus of Nazareth* which they remembered, the disciples put the *features of the Risen Lord* as they began to discover them after Easter, the glorious visage of the living Lord in their midst. When the gospels are read too naively, all seems clear: Jesus presents himself as the Son of God; Peter and the centurion shout it; we can only shake our heads in amazement at the Jews' not accepting him. Everything is, indeed, clear for us, because we are looking at all the drawings at the same time! For his contemporaries Jesus was primarily a question and an invitation. Faith is necessary, the light of Easter, the illumination of the Spirit, in order to see something of the richness of his mystery. We must look sometimes at the drawings together and sometimes at each one individually.[1]

The image of Jesus which the gospels offer us is historically fundamentally trustworthy both in terms of its general framework and what concerns the recollection of many of the details about his person and activity. We know, for example that the early Church was concerned with distinguishing clearly between Jesus' words as known from tradition and its own instructions. Thus does Paul write to his Corinthian Christians, 'To the married I give the charge, *not I but the Lord*, that the wife should not separate from her husband... to the rest I say, *not the Lord*, that any brother has a wife who is an unbeliever, and she consents to live with him, he should not divorce her...' (1 Cor 7:10-12; cp 1 Cor 7:25; 11:23). Yet, basic historicity and the influence of a believing standpoint are continually interwoven. This is very much the case in a number of miracle stories. It belongs to the delicate and complex but extremely fascinating task of exegesis to disentangle the various layers. Not to confront the one with the other but to discover the legitimate continuity between the historical Jesus and the Christ of faith and to interpret it as well as we can. As Jacques Maritain put it, *'distinguer pour unir'* [distinguish to unite]. But this – to use the picturesque image of an exegete – is only possible in hand to hand combat with a bayonet against the texts in the arena of detailed exegesis. In any case, an 'all or nothing' attitude toward the gospels' historicity is an extremely bad hermeneutical principle. The truth is that the gospels contain many facts which really happened and words which were really spoken as well as many that did not and were not.

Studies on the historical Jesus can fill libraries. It is impossible within the confines of this book to even try to give some idea of the problems that arise. We have already said that only those who know little of the question or who absolutely want to defend an apologetic position can present a polished and clear image of Jesus' figure and activity and of the conflicts which led to his execution. In reality, very many historical details and especially inter-connections remain (permanently) in the dark. An important cause, of course, is the fact that the gospels cannot be accepted formally as biography. But it is useful, as background for the further explanation, to list a few facts about Jesus.

Jesus of Nazareth was most likely *born* between 7 and 4 BC, during the last years of the rule of Herod the Great who died in 4 BC. (The Christian calendar, devised in 525 by the Roman priest Dionysius Exiguus, miscalculated by 4 to 7 years.) Jesus' birthplace was probably Bethlehem, although, seen from a purely historical point of view, this is less certain than his surrounding area, Nazareth in Galilee. Nazareth recalls no symbolic and theological associations; whereas Bethlehem could be connected with the witness that Jesus was the Son of David and King of Israel. David's roots were in Bethlehem. But this is not sufficient to deny that Jesus was born in Bethlehem.

About the *first thirty years of Jesus' life* we know as good as nothing. Even for historical science this period is literally Jesus' 'hidden life'. This of course largely explains why in all periods of christendom attempts were made to fill up these years. These attempts bring to light two main centres of interest. The first is to satisfy curiosity. From the second century onward, this impulse led to the existence of apocryphal infancy narratives in which (sometimes magnificent) folk legends about Jesus and his family arose. The second was the filling of this hidden period with a supposed and fantasized 'secret education', in order to explain how a carpenter's son from Nazareth could reach such deep religious insights. These are to be found mostly in the gnostic and esoteric interpretation of the Jesus figure. We do have a number of important and nearly certain data on the life and the historical condition in Palestine for this period. Thus the Roman domination, the socio-cultural and economic situation, the religious classes and movements (Sadducees, Pharisees, Essenes, Zealots), the tense apocalyptic atmosphere and the like shed much light on the framework in which Jesus lived and later would operate publicly. The literature from Qumran (the famous Dead Sea scrolls) and the inter-testamental writings (the so-called apocrypha and pseudepigrapha of the Old Testament) offer a treasure of information on the religious climate in Palestine and assist in the better understanding of many New Testament texts. But – and this is true of all historical data! – the historical value of a witness or recollection in the gospels must be weighed text per text and story per story.

During the high priesthood of Joseph, called Caiaphas (18-36) and the prefectship of Pontius Pilate (procurator) in Judaea (26-36) Jesus *operated in public* for a certain period, in which he gathered disciples and concentrated a good number of messianic expectations around his person. His activities, whose beginnings are historically anchored by other texts (particularly the Jewish historian Flavius Josephus) to the known figure of John the Baptist, can only have been of brief duration. Jesus was apparently swiftly liquidated. The Christian tradition speaks of a public life of three years on the basis of John's gospel in which Jesus celebrates at least three passovers.[2] It is generally accepted that these three years must have been a maximum. The synoptic gospels present it differently. There Jesus comes only once to Jerusalem, namely, a week before his death. If we had had only the first three gospels, we could easily put Jesus' public life within the period of one year. How quickly Jesus' fame grew and how long it took before he was found sufficiently dangerous to be eliminated is for historians a still unsolved problem.

During his public life Jesus had an unusual impact on the people he met. The question we meet so often in the gospel, 'who is that man?', doubtless reflects a correct historical recollection. See, for example, Mk 8:27-30. Many thought him a prophet and a large part of the messianic expectations prevalent in that period were directed toward him. Of course, this impact was brought about by what he *said and did*. In both ways he aroused great amazement. The comment in Mt 7:28-29, which can also be found in Mk 1:27-28, certainly conceals an historical recollection, 'And when Jesus finished these sayings, the crowds were astonished at his teaching...' Mark clearly indicates the two areas of amazement, a *new teaching with authority* and *he commands even the unclean spirits*. As far as this latter is concerned, it is as good as certain that Jesus acted as a healer and performed deeds interpreted by his contemporaries (friend and foe) as miracles, as special deeds of power. Texts such as Mt 12:22-27 or Mk 3:1-6; 7:32-36; 8:22-26 point overwhelmingly in this direction. But that the representation of Jesus as performer of miracles rests on a firm historical basis does not mean that *all* the miracles stories in the gospels can be treated in the same hermeneutical way. The opinion of the German bishop Walter Kasper puts into words the general consensus:

> Even after a critical investigation of the miracle traditions in the gospels, it appears impossible to argue against the wonder traditions' historical kernel. Jesus performed unusual deeds which astonished his contemporaries. Among these are the healing of various illnesses and symptoms which were understood in that time to be signs of possession. The so-called nature miracles, on the other hand, should most likely not be considered historical.[2]

During a passover week, Jesus of Nazareth was taken prisoner, *condemned* and delivered to the Roman authorities who *crucified* him. Many exegetes believe that the immediate incentive for this must have been the turmoil caused by his unprecedented behaviour in the temple which – particularly during the always already tense passover period – the authorities considered dangerous. It is not historically clear how far Jesus' fame had already penetrated Jerusalem nor how far he was considered there to be a potentially subversive element even before this behaviour. (Did Jesus enter Jerusalem as a king? If so, what was the scope of this demonstration?)

The *date* of Jesus' death cannot be determined with certainty. It must have been a passover day or a preparation day but the year remains undecided. There is a well-grounded preference (but no strict proof) favouring 3 April 33 or 7 April 30.[3]

Much research is being done on the question of the exact *motives* why Jesus was killed. The last word has not been spoken on this nor on what happened exactly at his trial. The reason for this is that the gospels describe Jesus' trial in function of their confession of faith rather than to serve the historian looking for hard facts. In general, we can agree with the following position: the cause of Jesus' condemnation and death was in essence a religious conflict which could have developed political repercussions and which was therefore politically resolved. We join the authors who posit that the heart of the matter was religious. Jesus was liquidated as a subversive element. In this sense he was well understood, for his views on God and man were indeed highly subversive for the established religious powers. What he said about and his relationship to the Torah were in some ways suspect when compared with the official interpretation of those versed in the law who were predominantly Pharisees. His forgiving, liberating, merciful contact with all who 'did not belong' – he ate with sinners and tax collectors, touched the impure, pointed to Samaritans and pagans as examples of true faith, etc. – confounded the criteria for a religious classification of people. His behaviour contravenes the criteria people used to decide who belonged with God and who did not. His radical freedom before all human institutions, because he was only concerned with obedience to God's will, must have unavoidably been regarded as highly dangerous for all who tried to cultivate their own power through the exercise of religious (and political) authority.

It is of course already an element of theological interpretation when we posit that Jesus' most 'dangerous' characteristic was his absolute and consistent rejection of *every* idol. But in our view it belongs to the core of his historical appearance and forms the real, most fundamental – be it perhaps unconscious – point of conflict with the religious authorities. who condemned him to death. The close connection between the religious authorities (especially the group of Sadducees around the high priest) and the political powers, meant that Jesus became a threat to both. The continuous interaction between the religious order and the Roman order facilitated handing Jesus over to the political authorities. Pilate was most likely empowered with the so-called *ius gladii* which means that the execution of capital punishment depended on his decision. For him personally the crucifixion of Jesus was probably no more that a boring news item, but the motive found in the gospels, namely, that he was brought to fear for his position before Caesar can very well refer to an historical recollection. Pilate was not a good governor, his position with Tiberius Caesar was far from stable.

After Jesus' death a number of events took place which aroused among the immediate disciples and among others who had known him the firm conviction that their teacher was *risen*, i.e. raised from the dead by God. For them this event – referred to in the gospel in the appearance narratives – was decisive for their belief in Jesus as Messiah. What had remained a question during his life – a question which had received a negative answer in his excommunication and death; note the disappointed words of the travellers to Emmaus in Lk 24:19-21, 'But we had hoped he was the one to redeem Israel...' – was now answered positively by God himself, God elevated Jesus of Nazareth to the Lord who fulfilled all Israel's messianic 'titles': Son of David, Son of God, King of Israel, in short, the Messiah, the Christ. What the real meaning is of Jesus' resurrection is a question which has been central to Christian theology for the past nineteen centuries. It is a basic question in christology, the teaching about Christ, as well as in the teaching on salvation, for Christ's resurrection is the cornerstone of Christian faith. Faith in the resurrection has nothing to do with a 'returning spirit'.

61

But it had everything to do with the belief that God's liberating self-revelation took definitive shape in Jesus and also works further there, not as pure recollection, but concretely and for so long as the world lasts. From the very beginning the Church, following the disciples' examples, did not accept Christ's resurrection as a metaphor (imagery), but as full reality, even if it could only be inadequately expressed in imagery. How life in God's glory, on the other side of death, could be, cannot be taught us by any resurrection story. In this sense, the resurrection stories have no informative value. It is not possible within the confines of this introduction to study the theological problems of the resurrection. To explain the gospel tradition's point of departure, it is sufficient here to note the fact that *faith in the resurrection* had without any doubt led to the proclamation of Jesus as the Christ and that in this sense it lies at the basis of the gospel tradition as such. Without the disciples' belief in the resurrection, there is a real possibility that we would have learned little or nothing of the existence of Jesus of Nazareth.

Jesus' disciples

The disciples who knew Jesus before his death became the first and immediate bearers of what was told and preached about Jesus, i.e. of the Jesus tradition. Robrecht Michiels correctly writes that we must attribute a two-fold characteristic to these disciples:

As authoritative personal witnesses they *guarantee*, on the one hand, that the *historical Jesus* really stands at the starting point of the gospel tradition about Jesus. At the same time Jesus' original disciples were able to provide an authentic *witness* to the *meaning* of the historical Jesus for *salvation*. Because they lived with Jesus for an extended period, they could sense the salvation historical import of Jesus' human words, through which, for them, God himself spoke, and of his human deeds, through which God himself acted. Although the disciples doubtless did not understand everything during Jesus' life and although they came to view a number of things differently in the light of the resurrection – a fact which will influence the tradition – their witness need not necessarily cloud the historical Jesus-event. On the contrary, it can also explain and clarify, just as ordinary historical facts must be explained and clarified, if they are to be 'meaning-ful' facts.[4]

It is extremely important to realize that Jesus' first disciples did not proclaim their master in the form of a biography. The heart of their message was that, by virtue of the resurrection, they confessed the crucified and rejected Jesus as Lord and Messiah. The heart of their call was a call to conversion and faith in the good news of the definitive breakthrough of God's loving and liberating self-revelation in Jesus Christ, or put dif-ferently, the definitive (eschatological) dawning of the kingdom of God. Of course, the preaching of Jesus as the risen Lord and Messiah had to refer to his historical appearance and activity in Galilee and Judea. They had to proclaim *who* it was who was confessed to be the crucified and risen Messiah. Many New Testament scholars are convinced that Peter's speech in Acts 10:34-43 contains a remarkable summary of the structure of the oldest proclamation.

You know the word which he [God] sent to Israel preaching good news of peace by Jesus Christ (he is the Lord of all), the word which was proclaimed throughout all Judea, beginning from Galilee after the baptism which John preached: how God anointed Jesus of Nazareth with the Holy Spirit and with power; how he went about doing good and healing all who were oppressed by the devil, for God was with him. And we are witnesses to all that he did both in the country of the Jews and in Jerusalem. They put him to death by hanging him on a tree; but God raised him on the third day and made him manifest; not to all the people but to us who were chosen by God as witnesses, who ate and drank with him after he rose from the dead. And he commanded us to preach to the people, and to testify that he is the one ordained by God to be judge of the living and the dead. To him all the prophets bear witness that every one who believes in him receives forgiveness of sins through his name.

The recollection of Jesus' words and deeds will not have been called up in the early Church in a systematically reconstructed biographical framework, but gradually, in small units and completely in function of the call to faith. We find other traces of the structure and content of the oldest proclamation in the so-called 'mission discourses' in the Acts of the Apostles. See, among other places, Acts 2:22-41; 3:13-26; 17-39. However these discourses have all been editorially reworked by Luke, as was the passage just quoted from Acts 10:36-43.

One of the most convincing illustration of the fact the oldest preachers and Church communities were not particularly interested in a continuous biography of Jesus can be found in Paul's letters. Paul, whose writings are the oldest Christian documents – the apostle had already died when the first of our present gospels saw the light of day! – never in his numerous teachings and instructions to his faithful tells stories about Jesus. In a manner of speaking, he mentions Christ only from the central point of cross and resurrection, and when he refers to words or traditions about Jesus, he always does it in function of the confession of faith and the concrete problems in his Churches. This does not diminish the fact that Paul too will have heard of the historical Jesus and would have told about him in his oral preaching.

The Christian communities between 30 and 70 AD

The Christian communities between the years 30 and 70 AD played a not to be underestimated role as *inheritors* of the tradition of the historical Jesus. In oral preaching and later in written tradition, the primitive Christian Church crystallized the recollection of Jesus. It did this from the fundamental concern to remain faithful to these traditions; and, as was already said, oral tradition can be surprisingly persistent and faithful. But in transmitting Jesus the Church doubtless worked creatively to a certain degree: adapting, up-dating, selecting in function of the Church's concrete situation... Synoptic research (see below, chapter 4) has demonstrated this beyond any doubt. The Churches were led in this process by an attitude of *double faithfulness*: *faithfulness to Jesus and faithfulness to life*,[5] a life which, within the Jewish and gentile world of the time, called up many questions and problems for the newborn Christian communities. The recollection of Jesus' words and deeds were not distributed among these communities to benefit neutral historical interest or to satisfy a curiosity for anecdotes. They have a practical and immediate function within the Church's life. The recollections about Jesus took shape primarily within three centres of interest.

1. *Preaching*. The disciples preached to bring the risen Christ to Jews and gentiles by proclaiming the good news, confessions and formulas of faith, calls to faith and conversion... In function of this preaching (thus also of 'proselytizing'), the *beatitudes*, for example, where Jesus proclaimed the breakthrough of God's dominion of love, mercy and justice, would be recalled; or the *miracle stories* which witness to his dominion over the powers of good and evil would be recounted; or there would be a retelling of the *parables* where the coming of the kingdom of God was related but where also there is a summons to commitment and radical choice, to faith and perseverance.

2. *Liturgy*. The first Church communities celebrated the risen Lord in growing and then gradually fixed liturgical forms, especially baptism and the celebration commemorating the Lord's Supper. In the framework of this liturgical celebration, fixed formulas of faith and confession (hymns, acclamations, etc.) grew. It is also in this context that narrative memories about Jesus would receive their fixed form, texts such as the *passion narrative* – which, like the Jewish Exodus narrative, would be told primarily with its symbolic, in-depth dimension in mind, as a sort of Christian 'Easter haggada'[6] – or also the stories around the *multiplication of the loaves*, which received clear eucharistic colouring.

3. *Catechesis and admonition*. The disciples and preachers taught the newly baptised and urged them to live consistently in

the path of Christ. This raised many concrete questions of faith as well as ethical problems which are often answered by referring to Jesus' example and words: How must we pray? Is fasting necessary? Is divorce allowed? Is contact with non-believers allowed? Can we eat anything or are there, for us too, impure foods we must avoid? May gentiles be included in our Church and under what conditions? What with forgiveness? What is our future, ultimately? Is Christ's return, is the final judgement close at hand? What with those who have already died? etc. In this framework many of Jesus' *controversies* and *teachings* will be recalled as will many *parables* (e.g. on the themes of legislation, perseverance, confidence under oppression, gradual and hidden growth of God's kingdom). Even *miracle stories* (e.g. quieting the storm – 'why are you afraid, you of little faith? – as a lesson to Christians in difficulty). It is fascinating, when comparing the gospels, to note the differences in the shared basic tradition. We see in them a permanent illustration of the *two-fold faithfulness* we already mentioned.

In this period – probably after the years 45 or 50 – the first writings of Christian literature were produced. The oldest preserved writings of the New Testament are Paul's letters, edited around the years 50 to 60. But it is very likely, to avoid saying absolutely sure, that a number of now lost writings saw the light of day in this period. They were of capital importance for fixing the traditions about Jesus and lay at the basis of our present gospels. Exegesis speaks here of a 'pre-synoptic' or 'pre-gospel' literary tradition. We think in particular of two types of documents:

– a primitive *passion narrative* read and used in the communities and existing in several versions.

– a collection of 'Jesus' sayings', i.e. words of Jesus which likely served as a vademecum in preaching and catechesis and also existing in slightly differing versions. We call this collection (of which we will speak further when discussing the synoptic question) by the German name *Logienquelle* (literally, words or sayings source) or simply *Quelle*, abbreviated Q.[7]

Composing the gospels

The actual composition of the gospels is best placed between the years 70 and 100. More on this later. This composition marks the final phase in the development of the traditions about Jesus. Here the *crystallizing* of the traditions and the authors' own *editorial work* are combined in a new synthesis.

Crystallizing the tradition in genres

The tradition about Jesus' words and deeds which had remained in principle faithful to the historical Jesus, but which also reflected various situations and problems in the young Church, gradually became crystallized in a number of *stereotypical* forms. In a manner of speaking, the stories about Jesus were poured in a mould where they more or less hardened. This means that similar types of stories came to be told in similar ways. (Good example are the stories about the calling of the apostles in Mk 1:16-18,19-20; 2:14; cp Lk 9:59-60.) In this way *genres* were gradually created for the New Testament, or were adopted from the Old Testament or from what is called 'intertestamental literature', i.e. Jewish writings from the period between the Old and New Testaments but not included in the biblical canon. That traditions take on a fixed form is a widely spread phenomenon. We recognize legends, fairy tales, sagas, jokes etc. primarily because they are structured in the same way and use the same linguistic form. Think of the fairy tales which all begin with 'Once upon a time' or the letters beginning with 'Dear' and ending with 'sincerely' or 'best wishes'. The formation of genres recognizable by their similar structure – even though a great freedom can be exercised within the structure – is a general fact of human expression. Think of music: sonata, fugue, opera, waltz... they are all genres recognizable by their structure. How can we distinguish between rock and blues except for characteristics of genre? Or in architecture: why do we immediately recognize that a church is a church and a castle a castle? Is a Church not an architectural 'genre'? Or think of the western in films, the landscape or still-life in art. The formation of genres is found in all branches of art.

The different fixed forms or genres of the gospel tradition have been a specific subject of research for what is known under the German name *Formgeschichte* [form criticism], i.e. the branch of biblical criticism which, as the name says, studies the history of the (anonymous) biblical linguistic forms. This method actually dates from the romantic period when the nineteenth century students of literature and language began investigating folk traditions and literature. It was the time of figures such as the brothers Grimm with their collection of folk takes. The simple popular linguistic forms or genres (saga, legend, fable, proverb, song, etc.) was classified as 'minor literature', i.e. literature not belonging to the 'great' authors but one in which individual authorship had less importance than its being collectively rooted in its culture or social group. The classical nineteenth century 'source criticism' was mainly occupied with locating documents which could be attributed to one single author or school and which served as source material for the present biblical document. Around the turn of the century there grew a view – especially under the influence of the German exegete Herman Gunkel – that many Old Testament passages did not derive from particular authors but must be considered '*einfache Formen*' ('simple forms'; the German refers to the title of a well known book by André Jolles published in 1930) and that they often had a more anonymous, collective and folk origin than had previously been supposed. Genesis contains a whole series of anonymous tribal and family sagas. Via Old Testament research, the *formgeschichtliche Methode* or *Formgeschichte* (beside the precise German terms, the terms 'form criticism' or 'form-critical method' are also used) entered New Testament studies. It became clear (Martin Dibelius and Rudolf Bultmann were the pioneers here) that the New Testament also owes a debt to anonymous and collective, simple and crystallizing linguistic forms.[8]

In studying the gospels we can make a rough division into *sayings* (i.e. *Jesus' words* or utterances; in these sayings Jesus is himself speaking) and *narrative material* (i.e. stories *about* Jesus). The borderline between these two is not always easily drawn – there are many of Jesus' words in narrative passages – but as a whole they still form the two main currents of the gospel tradition. Except for the passion narrative – which, of course, belongs to the narrative material – the sayings seem to be the oldest current of the biblical tradition, or at least to be the oldest vehicle of preaching and catechesis. This means that Jesus' words were used first and only later were stories told about him more systematically – stories often serve only as a framework to introduce Jesus' words. For this reason we can say that the sayings contain the most faithfully preserved elements of the Jesus tradition. Yet the narrative material has more or less come to predominate in the gospel tradition and has, for the most part, absorbed the sayings. That is why the gospels appear to be more 'stories about Jesus' than 'collections of Jesus' sayings'.

Within the sayings and narrative material the exegetes distinguish various genres, each with its own literary characteristics. Some of these genres have to do with Jesus' own way of speaking; others can be attributed to the influence of life in the young Church, with its adaptation and updating of the tradition; and still others may have been included by the evangelists themselves during their editorial work.

≥ 1. Among the sayings we can distinguish primarily:

– Jesus' *prophetic* sayings. These are sayings of Jesus which, in form and content, resemble the Old Testament prophets. We distinguish 'heraldic sayings' (e.g. Mt 1:15), prophetic accusations and warnings (e.g. Mk 7:5-13 or Mt 23:13-39), prophetic admonitions and calls to listen and be converted (e.g. Mt 13:9; 19:12).

– *Apocalyptic* sayings. These are sayings in the apocalyptic genre as is found in the book of Daniel or the Jewish apocryphal writings (e.g. Jesus' 'apocalyptic discourse' in Mt 24, Mk 13 and Lk 21). The apocalyptic style is often closely related to the prophetic.

– *Wisdom sayings*, in which Jesus speaks in the style of the Jewish sages, a sort of proverb which succinctly describes some aspect of life (e.g. Mk 6:4; Mt 10:24 or 25:23). There are also

69

warnings (e.g. Mt 6:25,34) and felicitations generally in the form of 'beatitudes' or, from the Greek word for blessed, makarisms (e.g. Mt 5:3-12). The expression 'Happy/Blessed is he who...' can also be found in the later Old Testament literature (cf Sir 25:8-9; Ps 1:1-2; 84:5-6).

– *Legal interdictions*, in which Jesus speaks in the style of a doctor of the law according to Old Testament and late-Jewish legal traditions (e.g. Mk 2:27; 10:11-12; Mt 5:18-19).

– *I sayings*. This type of saying seems much more typical of Jesus himself than those listed above. They are sayings in which Jesus, very formally, reveals something about his identity or person. In the synoptic gospels they generally take the form, 'I have (not) come to...'(e.g. Mk 2:17; Mt 10:34; Lk 12:49). In John, the I sayings will become a real systematic procedure to reveal Jesus' identity and will even crowd out the parables (e.g. Jn 6:35,41,48,51; 8:12,58; 10:7,11). When we discuss John's gospel later on, we will come back to these 'I am' sayings.

– *Parables*. Doubtless we touch here Jesus' most typical way of speaking. The parable genre is not unknown in the Old Testament and in rabbinic circles – think of Nathan's magnificent parable on the occasions of David's adultery with Bathsheba and Uriah's murder in 2 Samuel 12:1-4, or the 'Song of the vineyard' in Isaiah 5:1-7 – but Jesus seems to have had a special preference for this genre in proclaiming his message on the kingdom of God. Within the parable genre we can distinguish several sub-genres, each of which requires its own interpretation: the *comparisons* in the strict sense, expressly introduced with words like, 'the kingdom of God is like...' (e.g. Mk 4:26-29,30-23; Mt 13:31-34); the *parable* proper which is more of a continuous story (e.g. Mk 4:3-9; 12:1-12; Lk 14:16-24; 15:11-32); the *example*, primarily intended as a lesson to be imitated (e.g. Lk 10:25,29-37; 12:16-21; 18:9-14); the *allegory* in which the story's various details have a hidden meaning (e.g. Mt 13:18-23,36-43).

The sayings bring us into contact with Jesus himself – many sayings have been passed on to us faithfully preserved and extremely intact – but also in contact with the life of the young Church. Tradition and the evangelists have taken the words of

Jesus and up-dated and adapted them to a greater or lesser extent. That is why these sayings not only shed light on Jesus himself, but also on the situation in the early Church communities *and* on the evangelists' own theology. Compare, for example, what Jesus says about divorce in Mk 10:11 (1 Cor 7:10-11!) with Mt 5:32 and 19:9. The clause on the exception for adultery probably reveals the situation in the Matthean Church. Compare also Mt 25:14-30 with Lk 19:11-27. The evangelists have put the parable on the talents (pounds) within different contexts in their gospels. Matthew gives it a somewhat different theological meaning than Luke. In Matthew the text refers immediately to the text of the Last Judgement and is therefore (together with the parable of the bridesmaids) an urgent call to be on guard against the coming end. In Luke, Jesus tells the parable to warn his disciples not to 'suppose that the kingdom of God was to appear immediately' (Lk 19-11). Jesus' kingship will not be accepted by his countrymen; only later will he receive the kingship. The parable (which has something of an allegory to it in vv. 12-15) is also a warning for the Christians of Luke's time. Rather than tensely awaiting the immanent appearance of the kingdom of God, they must now, while their king is not with them, perform their task to their fullest ability. ≤

≥ 2. Within the narrative material we distinguish:
– what are called *sayings narratives*. These narratives, very characteristic of the gospels, are stories whose main interest lies in the pronouncement of the Lord used to make the point of the story. We find here primarily controversies and instructions. *Controversies* place Jesus up against his opponents and end with one of his sayings on one or other subject (mainly over the interpretation of the Torah, e.g. Mk 2:15-28; 12:13-27; as we will see further in this book, in John the controversies can grow into discussions that fill several pages). In the *instructions* we hear Jesus, in the framework of a short story not located in a specifically controversial context, speak to teach his disciples (e.g. Mk 3:31-35; 10:13-51; Lk 10:38-42). A special type of sayings narrative (we also call these discourse narratives) are the *calling of the disciples*. These short stories offer a

71

stereotypically told situation which ends in Jesus' call and the immediate reaction of the one called. Typical examples are Mk 1:1-16-18,19-20; 2:13-14. Note that Mark has the most original and most purely preserved genres (see the discussion on his gospel below).

– The *miracle stories* form an important category of narratives. There is much discussion among exegetes on their origin, age and division. What *is* certain is that the miracle stories, originally based on historical recollections, have undergone an *evolution* in which preaching (*kerygma*) and theological intentions strongly colour and sometimes supplant the historical recollections. There is a long period of evolution between a simple exorcism story and a strongly symbolic story such as the marriage at Cana in John! Among the miracle stories we distinguish by and large the following groups: *healing stories* (e.g. Mk 1:40-45; 2:1-12; 7:31-37); *exorcisms* (e.g. Mk 1:23-28; 9:14-27); *nature miracles* (e.g. Mk 4:35-41; 6:35-44); and *raisings from the dead* (e.g. Mk 5:21-24,35-43; Lk 7:11-17; Jn 11:1-44). It is generally accepted that the exorcisms and healing stories reflect the oldest miracle traditions and recollections. Nature miracles and raisings are 'younger', in the sense that they are more thoroughly coloured by the post-Easter theological view. They have occasionally become genuine theologically christological stories which grew as illustrations of the glory of the risen Lord who gives life and has power over all creation.

– What is known as *Word of God stories* also form a separate genre within the narrative material. Here the central point is not one of Jesus' sayings or powerful deeds, but a witness about Jesus addressed to the people. This enunciation from God about Jesus can take the form of a voice from heaven (e.g. at the baptism, Mk 1:9-11; at the transfiguration, Mk 9:2-8), or the message of an angel (e.g. the infancy narratives, Mt 1:18-23; Lk 1:11-20, 1:26-37; 2:8-14; the stories around the empty tomb, Mt 29:1ff; Lk 24:4ff). A dream can also serve this function (as Joseph's dream in Mt 1:20; 2:13,19). The Word of God stories are very strongly influenced by Old Testament and apocalyptic methods of making God's revelation known. Especially in the inter-testamental literature, which was very successful and influential in the first century, heavenly visions and oracles are frequent beside continuous messages from angels. What is called *Angelus interpres* or the 'explaining angel' (as with the shepherds at Bethlehem or the empty tomb) is an accepted literary device in apocalyptic literature.[9] In the gospel, the Word of God stories are a way to express that Jesus' mission has God's approval or, more simply, they tell us what God thinks or has to say about Jesus. The evangelists' frequent references to the fulfilment of the Scriptures have more or less the same function as the Word of God stories. They too are a way to put God's 'ratifying signature' on Jesus' words and deeds. The reference to fulfilling the Scriptures locates Jesus within God's plan of salvation. Taken globally, the Word of God stories (not the references to Scripture) are the *youngest branch* of the narrative material. The sayings are the oldest, while the miracle stories are in between. ≤

– The *passion narrative* stands apart as a genre in the formation of the gospel tradition. It belongs to what is known as 'historical narrative', a genre well known from the Old Testament, combining real historical recollections with theological and symbolic explanation. As will be explained further on in this book, the passion narrative is the oldest and most important part, the heart of the written gospels.

– Finally, there are also the *infancy narratives* found only in Matthew and Luke, in two very different versions. The infancy narratives are in a certain sense the most 'theological' stories in the gospels. The evangelists added them as a sort of entrance way to the gospel in order, imitating the style of Old Testament predictions about great figures, to summarize the meaning of Jesus. The infancy narratives offer very little historical information, but are very important for christology. They want to make perfectly clear *who* Jesus of Nazareth is and what his place is in God's order of salvation. They fulfil more or less the same function as the prologue to John's gospel, but the style they use to do this is completely different. The infancy narratives, in style most closely related to the Old Testament, used a genre dear to Jewish rabbinical circles, the *haggada midrash*. This was (and is) a manner of applied explanation of the Scripture where new stories are built using old biblical stories and a variety of other scriptural 'material'. Using words, terms, persons, stories and situations from the Bible, stories are built to explain the meaning of the present (for the evangelists, Jesus) against a scriptural background. In the Old Testament, the books of Ruth and Jonah belong more or less to this genre (see note 6). Christian exegesis' 'rediscovery' of this Jewish way to explain the Bible has led to a growing consensus that the infancy narratives (just as theAscension and Pentecost narratives in Acts) are examples of Christian 'haggada'. They are for the most part Christian midrash stories. Using Old Testament, Jewish (and even Hellenistic) material, Matthew and Luke create strong, theologically well-considered stories which announce and determine the christology of their gospels. Matthew does this against the backdrop of the history of the People of God, which he sees summarized in Jesus (e.g. Israel in Egypt), Luke mainly against the background of Old Testament announcement and nativity stories (cf Lk 1:11-20 and 1:26-37 with Judg 6:11-24 and 13:1-25; cf Lk 1:46-56 with 1 Sam 2:1-10). The so-called apocryphal gospels often used the midrash method. They took materials from the canonical gospels and the Old Testament to form new stories.

An important remark must be added to this concise overview of the narrative material. The fact that a gospel offers a series of stories and also as a whole appears in the form of a story, has a meaning for the interpretation of revelation which should not be underestimated. Stories tell what *happened* with and around Jesus. A gospel – just as the Old Testament – lets us know implicitly that God not only reveals himself in spoken words, but also and even essentially in what happens! In other words, the stories in the gospels teach us that *Jesus' own actions*, what he did and what he brought about, is God's revelation. The Good News is not only the words he spoke, but his activity, his healing, liberating, forgiving activity is itself God's good news for humanity. Jesus is also a story Jesus is gospel as event. With this insight – the insight of what is called 'narrative theology' – we come close to the explanation given in chapter 2. The summary of the gospel cited on p. 63, says with reason '[You know]... how he went about doing good and healing all that were oppressed by the devil... We are witnesses to *all that he did* in the country of the Jews...' (Acts 10:37-39).

The writing process

All the material mentioned above (the oral Jesus traditions which circulated separately in the communities; the first written documents) arrived ultimately by various people who will use them to construct the gospels as we know them. How the evangelists relate to one another is the subject of 'synoptic research' or the 'synoptic question', but even here we can already say that *Mark* in all likelihood may be called the 'designer' or 'creator' of the sort of book that we now call gospel. He penned his gospel (the first, thus) most likely between the years 66 and 73. Matthew and Luke wrote their gospels in the years 80-90. John probably wrote between 95 and 100.

The evangelists find themselves in the middle of a tradition already several decades old. They work using material that they *did not themselves design*. The substrata of their editorial work consist in anonymous traditional material; partly crystallized in the pre-literary narrative forms or genres, which they had learned in their Church communities. In this sense the evangelists are not creative authors but *collectors*. Yet they did leave a very clear imprint on the Scriptures; in their arrangement of the material, their additions and deletions, their own editorial contribution and creativity we see signs of their own theology, their own view of Jesus Christ. Evangelists are in all respects *interpreters* of the Jesus tradition.

It is no accident that the gospels were born in the last third of the first century. This period is characterized by what is called the 'problems of the second and third generations'. For a number of Christians the enthusiasm of the first years had dimmed somewhat. They were tired. The 'end of times' announced to them kept them waiting. The Church had already been confronted with apostasy partly under the pressure of difficulties and persecutions. The Church communities were also more and more confronted with diverging interpretations of the faith. Gnosis began to gain ground here and there. In this situation the demise of the first witnesses to Jesus was sorely felt. As the apostles and preachers of the first generation began to disappear the need grew to fix the apostolic tradition in writings which would form a permanent norm and safe criterion for the faith because they were still endowed with the authority of the apostolic teaching. The gospels may be considered an answer to this need. They want to guarantee a proclamation that is faithful to the apostles' original witness to Jesus' words and deeds, with the goal of preserving and transmitting the 'good news' authentically.

What then is a gospel?

Although the real answer to this question can only be found gradually through incessant reading of the gospel – and even more by living it, the gospel must become an existential reality – we have reached the point where we can formulate a usable description of the gospel as a literary genre.

Content and intention

According to their *content and intention* we may consider the gospels in the first place as *witnesses to faith* and *confessions of faith*. R. Michiels correctly notes that they were written from faith in service of faith. As we have already made clear, their goal is never neutrally informative, but committed and kerygmatic, i.e. devoted to preaching that Jesus was the Messiah. It is important to be aware here that the gospels were written in the first place for the Christian communities (thus, for 'intramural' use). They are not intended apologetically, to 'prove' to non-believers that Christ is God! The apologetic intention is only a secondary attribute (it is indeed present in a certain number of texts) and gained ascendancy in the Church's interpretation mainly after the

Enlightenment period. This has not seldom enshrouded the original meaning of many texts (in particular the miracle stories). R. Michiels writes:

The gospels do reflect 'historical' events and words, but they also witness to the meaning these words and deeds have for salvation. They clarify, elucidate, interpret and apply these words and deeds from a believing insight in the meaning the historical figure Jesus has for salvation; they look upon Jesus' words and deeds in the light of their belief in God and their confession of him. Our gospels are interested in Jesus' earthly historical existence, in his historical words and deeds, only in so far as they can be made to serve the first Christians' insight into and confession of faith. For these Christians, the historical Jesus is not imprisoned in a totally closed past nor is he evaporated in timelessness, but remains vibrantly present as the risen and glorified Lord; he speaks and acts and lives with his own until the end of time... Since the historical image of Jesus is built on the basis of or using a theological and christological conception, history and faith, facts and preaching, tradition and interpretation are inseparable in the early Church.[10]

Form

We can subscribe to the description of the gospels' form as formulated by P. Van den Berghe:

A gospel is a work that collects Jesus' words and stories about Jesus, arising from a living Church tradition and arranges them in a more or less closed biographical narrative of his acts, told in the light of his final days, and having as ultimate and decisive purpose to draw attention to what God himself has told us through Jesus and about Jesus.

Seen in terms of its form, a gospel is a *narrative* about what *happened* to Jesus (cf p. 74), a narrative that offers an in-depth reading of the events, i.e. it always has in mind the event under the events and demonstrates this in its dominating concern for what was *said*. The event itself is called 'Word', i.e. message about what God has done for mankind in Jesus Christ. In this sense perhaps we could succinctly describe the kind of book a gospel is by saying, a gospel is a biographical saying and revelation narrative. In this formulation, also borrowed from P. Van den Berghe, the word 'biographical' does not, of course, mean that the gospels were written primarily because of interest in Jesus' biography – this should be more than clear from all that has been said above – but that the gospel, as saying narrative, relates events from Jesus' life. The biographical element remains clearly subordinate to preaching and catechesis. What is told about Jesus is used *to serve witness, encouragement and admonition, the underpinning and defence of the faith, instruction and training*. This reflects the polyvalent purpose of a gospel.

At this point in our disquisition, it is fitting to insert a note on the gospels' *inspiration*. In the light of the preceding it is clear that we cannot take the concept 'inspiration' to mean a type of mechanical intervention by the Holy Spirit as a replacement for human mechanisms or methodologies, or for free human choice and selection. It is also evident that the concept inspiration must be applied to the gospel's own level of wisdom. Thus inspiration does not mean that the gospels are watertight and infallible on *all* levels (scientific, geographical, historiographical, etc.). That is by no means the case, and in that regard the New Testament differs very little from the Old. In the concept 'inspiration of the Holy Spirit', the Church expresses its belief that God's guarantee rests on the gospel's intended truth, i.e. on the gospels as vehicles of the truth about salvation. When we say that the gospels are inspired with regard to Jesus, we refer to the Christian conviction that the evangelists offer us an image of Jesus that puts into words in full truth the essence of his person, his message and his meaning (even when this happens via stories that did not 'really happen'). Put differently, the gospels offer the authentic image, guaranteed by God, of Jesus as God's Word, as the revelation of God's salvation on earth. In the light of all we have already said, we could also add to this as 'symbol' – or what amounts to the same thing, as sacrament – of God. It is also clear that we are speaking of a reality which cannot be 'scientifically proven'. Concepts such as 'inspiration of the Holy Spirit' move within a linguistic field where the question of proof is totally beside the point. It is as if we were to demand scientific proof that Mozart's *Requiem* is beautiful, or that someone's love for another is really true. Whoever reads the gospels primarily from this narrow apologetic – and when looked at closely, very rationalistic – perspective, fails to appreciate the essence of the believing attitude as an act of trust translated in existential commitment, i.e. in a way of life. Extrinsic 'proofs' of the faith serve ultimately only to remove the 'risk' present in any act of trust by positing that we 'know' that it is so because it 'has been historically proven' that Jesus was right, that he is God. Whoever analyses this position psychologically quickly meets the underlying fear to take the risk involved in believing. But these thoughts belong to another field of theology, namely, fundamental dogmatics. But it remains true that the correctness of faith can never be proven *a priori* and from outside. The experience of a wholeness which arises in the ever continuing confrontation of the gospel with a life of faith plays an irreplaceable and necessary role in the underpinning of that faith and this remains so, even when we speak of Scripture's inspiration.

NOTES

1   E. Charpentier, *Pour lire le Nouveau Testament* [*To read the New Testament*], Paris, 1981, p. 19. This translation follows the Dutch text which adapts the French somewhat for reasons of clarity.
2   Other elements from the gospels can also be called upon to support this duration, such as a 'biographical' interpretation of the parable Jesus tells in Lk 13:6-9 where the owner of the fig tree in the vineyard says, 'these *three years* I have come seeking fruit on this fig tree, and I find none.' The parable refers to efforts Jesus made in vain – cf Mk 11:12-14 – but whether the number *three* here can be read as an historical reference is by no means sure.

3   Other dates are also suggested (among them 27 or 34). The difficulty of the astronomical calculations in this regard is partly due to the fact that John does not agree with the synoptic authors in dating the crucifixion.

4   R. Michiels, *Evangelie en evangelies* [*Gospel and Gospels*], Leuven, 1986, p. 106. Here we touch the very difficult question of the relationship between historical factuality and its interpretation and equally of the possibility of an objective knowledge of history, as well as the problem of the relationship of language to reality. One of the important questions raised by Umberto Eco's *The Name of the Rose* is whether or not history is what we think and remember of it and what we say about it.

5   We borrow this formulation from E. Charpentier, *op. cit.*, p. 10.

6   The 'haggada' is originally a genre of rabbinical biblical exegesis belonging to what is called 'midrash'. The haggada's goal is to provide historical information and ethical instruction to serve a broad religious education. It is elevating and admonishing, but flexible and supple in its methodology. Through religious meditation, teaching and legend, piety and folklore, it fulfills the desire for a concrete application of the canonical biblical texts. The texts accompanying the Jewish passover celebration belong largely to the haggada genre. (We borrow this explanation from *Bijbels Woordenboek* [*Dictionary of the Bible*], 3rd ed., 1966-69, s.v.)

7   In recent years attempts have been made to reconstruct such a pre-gospel document working back from the existing gospels. Rudolf Pesch published in 1979 an *Evangelium der Urgemeinde* [*Gospel of the Primitive Church*] and Athenasius Polag produced a reconstruction of the *Quelle* in the same year. In 1988, a team of New Testament specialists in Leuven around Prof. Frans Neirynck even compiled a 'synopsis' of the *Quelle*, i.e. a comparative edition of two versions of this document, both distilled from the gospels of Matthew and Luke.

8   On this see, chapter 1, note 4. Whoever studies simple anonymous linguistic forms, swiftly comes in contact with the folk traditions on which they are based. This lead rather quickly to a development, from the form critical method, of a *traditionsgeschichtlich* [tradition historical] method or *Traditionsgeschichte* [history of traditions] which studies the formation and history of the various traditions interwoven in the biblical literature. We call this 'tradition criticism'. For the Old Testament this involves tribal and exodus traditions; for the New Testament we speak of Galilean traditions or Jerusalem traditions. As the form critical and tradition critical investigation advanced, interest grew in the way in which the final authors of our present texts used and integrated these genres and traditions. The study of the individual editorial activity of the sacred authors has become very important over the last thirty years, since it is from their personal editorial reworking of the traditional material that we can best learn about their own historical and theological views. The branch of biblical sciences which primarily studies the author's editorial activity is called *Redaktionsgeschichte*, 'redaction history or redaction criticism'.

9   ≥ Examples of visions, dreams and angelic messages from the inter-testamental literature cannot be given here. A few parallels from the Old Testament are Gen 28:10-19; 31:11-16,24; 37:5-11; 40:5-22; 41:1-36; Num 12:6; Dan 2:1-45; 4:1-24 (dreams); in the 'apocalypse of Daniel', Dan 7-12, there are

heavenly visions and voices in addition to declarations by angels (e.g. Gabriel in 9:21). New Testament parallels can be found in Acts 1:10-11; 2:2-3; 7:55-56; 8:26; 9:3-7 (par. 22:6-11; 26:13-16); 9:10,12; 10:3-8,9-16,30-31; 12:7-10; 16:9-10; 18:9; 22:17-18 and all through the book of the Apocalypse (Revelation). ≤

10 R. Michiels, *op. cit.*, p. 110f.

4

The synoptic question

Introduction: The name 'synoptic gospels'

Whoever reads through the whole of the four canonical gospels and compares them with one another, notes the striking characteristic of their mutual relationship. It is as if the gospels were divided in two teams with Matthew, Mark and Luke on the one side and while John is on his own on the other. The first three gospels show a great similarity over the whole line: the framework of their story, their presentation of Jesus, the reflection of his words and deeds, the general content – the main lines all generally agree. But John's gospel is clearly distinct from the other three: Jesus' public life is differently arranged in its chronological framework; John for a large part mentions other of Jesus' words and deeds; the style of Jesus' acts and deed is also strikingly different from that in the first three gospels. For all these reasons exegesis takes the first three gospels together and studies John's gospel separately. That is also what we will do in this introduction.

The first three gospels are called *synoptic gospels* (and their writers *synoptici*). The Greek word 'synopsis' means 'general overview', 'summarizing overview'. Because the first three gospels offer for a large part the same story of Jesus' life, words and deeds, it is possible to arrange or print the story in three columns side by side, so that we see at a glance an overview, a 'synopsis' of Jesus' life and activity . The name 'synoptic gospels' dates from the end of the eighteenth century. J. J. Griesbach first used this term in his work *Libri Historici Novi Testamenti Graece*, published in Halle in 1774. Griesbach is also the author of the first *synopsis*, i.e. a publication of the first three gospels in three parallel columns. Since then many synopses have been published, some even with a fourth column for John's gospel.[1] The synopsis has become an indispensable tool in biblical studies. The synoptic reading of the gospels has contributed greatly to the depth of our insight into this literature, on historical, literary and theological levels. The treatment of the synoptic question may justly be called *the* major accomplishment of nineteenth century New Testament exegesis. The present accumulation of knowledge on the growth and editing of the gospels is for a very large part due to synoptic research.

≥ With the agreement of the authors we reproduce here a number of pages of the English Bible texts using the layout found in the *Synopsis* by A. Denaux and M. Vervenne. Whether there is text provided or not, a synopsis *always* divides the page in three columns, one for each evangelist. The examples illustrate in sequence the triple, double and single tradition or *Sondergut*.

The triple tradition:

§67. THE HEALING OF A PALSIED MAN

Mt 9:1-8	Mk 2:1-12	Lk 5:17-26

1 And getting into a boat he crossed over	(§)
	   5:18 (§143)
		(§)
		   8:37 (143)

		17 On one of those days 7:1 (§109)
	1 And when he returned to Capernaum after some days, it was reported	
and came into his own city.	that he was at home.	
	2 And many were gathered together, so that there was no longer room for them, not even about the door; and he was preaching the word to them.	as he was teaching, there were Pharisees and teachers of the law sitting by who had come from every village of Galilee and Judea and from Jerusalem; and the power of the Lord was with him to heal.
	3:8 (§96)	
2 And behold, they brought to him a paralytic	**3** And they came bringing to him a paralytic	**18** And behold, men were bringing on a bed a man who was paralysed
lying on his bed,	carried by four men.	
		and they sought to bring him in and lay him before Jesus;
	And when they could not get near him because of the crowd, they removed the roof above him, and when they had made an opening,	but finding no way to bring him in, because of the crowd, they went up on the roof
	they let down the pallet on which the paralytic lay.	and let him down with his bed through the tiles into the midst before Jesus

and when Jesus saw their faith he said to the paralytic, 'Take heart, my son, your sins are forgiven.'	**5** And when Jesus saw their faith he said to the paralytic, My son, your sins are forgiven.'	**20** And when he saw their faith he said, 'Man, your sins are forgiven you.'
3 And behold, some of the scribes said to themselves,	**6** Now some of the scribes were sitting there, questioning in their hearts,	**20** And the scribes and the Pharisees began to question, saying,
	7 'Why does this man speak thus? It is blasphemy!	
'This man is blaspheming.'	Who can forgive sins but God alone?'	'Who is this that speaks blasphemies? 'Who can forgive sins but God only?'
4 But Jesus, knowing their thoughts,	**8** And immediately Jesus, perceiving in his spirit that they thus questioned within themselves,	**22** When Jesus perceived their questionings.
said, 'Why do you think evil in your hearts?'	said to them, 'Why do you question thus in your hearts?'	he answered them, 'Why do you question in your hearts?'
5 For which is easier, to say, 'Your sins are forgiven', or to say, 'Rise and walk'?	**9** Which is easier, to say to the paralytic, 'Your sins are forgiven', or to say, 'Rise, take up your pallet and walk'?	**23** Which is easier, to say, 'Your sins are forgiven you', or to say, 'Rise and walk'?
6 But that you may know that the Son of man has authority on earth to forgive sins' – he then said to the paralytic –	**10** But that you may know that the Son of man has authority on earth to forgive sins' – he said to the paralytic –	**24** But that you may know that the Son of man has authority on earth to forgive sins' – he said to the man who was paralysed –
'Rise, take up your bed and go home.'	**11** 'I say to you, rise, take up your pallet and go home.'	'I say to you, rise, take up your bed and go home.'
11 And when the Pharisees saw this,	**16** And the scribes of the Pharisees, when they saw that he was eating with sinners and tax collectors,	**30** And the Pharisees and their scribes

they said to his disciples,	said to his disciples,	murmured against his disciples, saying,
'Why does your teacher eat with tax collectors and sinners?'	'Why does he eat with tax collectors ands sinners?'	'Why do you eat and drink with tax collectors and sinners?'
12 But when he heard it, he said, 'Those who are well have no need of a physician, but those who are sick.	**17** And when Jesus heard it, he said to them, 'Those who are well have no need of a physician, but those who are sick.	**31** And Jesus answered them, 'Those who are well have no need of a physician, but those who are sick.
13 Go and learn what this means, 'I desire mercy, and not sacrifice.' (Hos 6:61) For I came not to call the righteous, but sinners.'	12:33b (§293) I came not to call the righteous, but sinners.'	**32** I have not come to call the righteous, but sinners to repentance.'

§70. THE QUESTION ABOUT FASTING. THE OLD AND THE NEW

Mt 9:14-17	Mk 2:18-22	Lk 5:33-39
14 Then the disciples of John	**18** Now John's disciples and the Pharisees were fasting;	**33** And they
came to him, saying, 'Why do we and the Pharisees	and people came and said to him, 'Why do John's disciples and the disciples of the Pharisees	said to him, 'The disciples of John
fast,	fast,	fast often and offer prayers, and so do the disciples of the Pharisees,
but your dsiciples do not fast?'	but your disciples do not fast?'	but yours eat and drink.'
15 And Jesus said to them, 'Can the wedding guests mourn as long as the bridegroom is with them?'	**19** And Jesus said to them, 'Can the wedding guests fast while the bridegroom is with them?' As long as they have the bridegroom with them, they cannot fast.	**34** And Jesus said to them, 'Can you make wedding guests fast while the bridegroom is with them?'

The days will come, when the bridegroom is taken away from them, and then they will fast.	**20** The days will come, whent he bridegroom is taken away from them, and then they will fast in that day.'	**35** The days will come, when the bridegroom is taken away from them, and then they will fast in those days.'
		36 He told them a parable also: 'No one tears a piece from a new garment and puts upon an old garment; if he does
16 And no one puts a piece of unshrunk cloth on an old garment;	**21** No one sews a piece of unshrunk cloth on an old garment;	
for the patch tears away from the garment	if he does, the patch tears away from it, the new from the old,	
and a worse tear is made.	and a worse tear is made.	he will tear the new, and the piece from the new will not match the old.
17 Neither is new wine put into old wineskins; if it is,	**22** And no one puts new wine into old wineskins; if he does, the wine will	**37** And no one puts new wine into old wineskins; if he does, the new wine will
the skins burst, and the wine is spilled, and the skins are destroyed; but new wine is put into fresh wineskins, and so both are preserved.'	burst the skins, and the wine is lost, and so are the skins. but new wine is for fresh skins.'	burst the skins and it will be spilled, and the skins will be destroyed. **38** But new wine must be put into fresh wineskins.
	(§94)	**39** And no one after drinking old wine desires new; for he says, "The old is good".'

The double tradition:

§20. THE TEMPTATION

Mt 4:2-9		Lk 4:2-7
2 And he fasted forty days and forty nights (Ex 24:18;1 Kings 19:8) and afterward he was hungry		**2b** and he ate nothing in those days and when they were ended, he was hungry.

3 And the tempter came
and said to him,
'If you are the Son of God,
command these stones
becomes loaves of bread.'

4 But he answered,
'It is written,
"Man shall not live
by bread alone,
but by every word
that proceeds from the
mouth of God".' (Dt 8:3)

5 Then the devil took him
to the holy city, and set him
on the pinnacle of the temple,

6 and said to him,
'If you are the Son of God,
throw yourself down;
for it is written,
"He will give his angels
charge of you"
and
"On their hands they will
bear you up lest you strike
your foot against a stone".'
(Ps 91:11f)

7 Jesus said to him,
'Again it is written,
"You shall not tempt
the Lord your God".'
(Dt 6:16)

8 Again, the devil took him
to a very high mountain,
and and showed him all the
kingdoms
of the world
and the glory of them;

9 and he said to him,
"All these
I will give you,

if you will fall down
and worship me."

---

3 The devil
said to him,
'If you are the Son of God,
command this stone
to become bread.'

4 And Jesus answered him
'It is written
"Man shall not live
by bread alone".' (Dt 8:13)

v. 9-12

5 And the devil took him
up,
and showed him all the
kingdoms
of the world
in a moment of time,

6 and said to him,
"To you I will give
all this authority
and their glory;
for it has been delivered
to me, and I give it to whom
I will.

7 If you, then,
will worship me,
it shall all be yours."

88

10 Then Jesus said to him,
'Begone, Satan!
for it is written,
"You shall worship
the Lord your God
and him only
shall you serve".'
(Dt 5:9; 6:13; 10:20)

11 And the devil left him,

and behold, angels came
and ministered to him.

and he was with the
wild beasts;
and the angels
ministered to him.

8 And Jesus answered him,

'It is written,
"You shall worship
the Lord your God,
and him only
shall you serve".'
(Dt 5:4; 6:13; 10:20)

9 And he took him
to Jerusalem,
and set him
on the pinnacle of the temple,
and said to him,
'If you are the Son of God,
throw yourself down from here

10 for it is written,
"He will give his angels
charge of you
to guard you,"

11 and "On their hands
they will bear you up,
lest you strike your foot
against a stone".' (Ps 91:11)

12 And Jesus answered him,
'It is said,
"You shall not tempt
the Lord your God".'

13 And when the devil
had ended every
temptation,
he departed from him
until an opportune time.

The single tradition or *Sondergut*

§37. ON ALMSGIVING

1 'Beware of practising your piety before men
in order to be seen by them;
for then you will have no reward from your Father who is in heaven.

2 Thus, when you give alms
sound no trumpet before you,
as the hypocrites do in the synagogues and in the streets,
that they may be praised by men.
Truly, I say to you, they have received their reward.

3 But when you give alms,
do not let your left hand know what your right hand is doing,

4 so that your alms may be in secret;
and your Father who sees in secret will reward you.'

§38. PRAYING

5 'And when you pray,
you must not be like the hypocrites;
for they love to stand and pray in the synagogues and at the street corners,
that they may be seen by men.
Truly, I say to you,
they have received their reward.

6 But when you pray,
go into your room and shut the door (Is 26:20 LXX; 2 Kings 4:3)
and pray to your Father who is in secret;
and your Father who sees in secret will reward you.'

§41. FASTING

16 And when you fast,
do not look dismal, like the hypocrites,
for they disfigure their faces that their fasting may be seen by men.
Truly, I say to you,
they have received their reward.

17 But when you fast,
anoint your head and wash your face,

18 that your fasting may not be seen by men
but by your Father who is in secret;
and your Father who sees in secret will reward you.'

§239. PARABLE OF THE LOST COIN

Mt   **Mk**   **Lk 15:8-10**

8 'Or what woman, having ten silver coins, if she loses one coin,
does not light a lamp and sweep the house
and seek diligently until she finds it?

9 And when she found it,
she calls together her friends and neighbours, saying
'Rejoice with me,
for I have found the coin which I had lost.'

10 Just so, I tell you, there is joy before the angels of God
over one sinner who repents.'

§240. PARABLE OF THE PRODIGAL SON

Lk 15:11-32

11 And he said,
'There was a man who had two sons;

12 and the younger of them said to his father,
"Father, give me the share of property that falls to me."
And he divided his living between them.

13 Not many days later, the younger son gathered all he had
and took his journey into a far country,
and there he squandered his property in loose living.

14 And when he had spent everything,
a great famine arose in that country,
and he began to be in want.

15 So he went and joined himself to one of the citizens of that country,
who sent him into his fields to feed swine.

16 And he would gladly have fed
on the pods that the swine ate;
and no one gave him anything.

17 But when he came to himself he said,
"How many of my father's hired servants have bread enough and to spare,
but I perish here with hunger!

18 I will arise and go to my father, and I will say to him,
"Father, I have sinned against heaven and before you;

19 I am no longer worthy to be called your son;
treat me as one of your hired servants".'

20 And he arose and came to his father.
But while he was yet at a distance,
his father saw him and had compassion,
and ran and embraced him and kissed him.

21 And the son said to him,
"Father, I have sinned against heaven and before you;
I am no longer worthy to be called your son."

22 But the father said to his servants,
"Bring quickly the best robe, and put it on him;
and put a ring on his hand, and shoes on his feet;

23 And bring the fatted calf and kill it,
and let us eat and make merry;

24 for this my son was dead, and is alive again;
he was lost, and is found."
And they began to make merry.

25 Now his elder son was in the field;
and as he came and drew near to the house,
he heard music and dancing.

26 And he called one of the servants
and asked what this meant.

27 And he said to him,
"Your brother has come,
and your father has killed the fatted calf,
because he has received him safe and sound."

28 But he was angry and refused to go in.
His father came out and entreated him,

29 but he answered his father,
"Lo, these many years I have served you,
and I never disobeyed your command,
yet you never gave a kid,
that I might make merry with my friends.

30 But when this son of yours came,
who has devoured your living with harlots,
you killed for him the fatted calf!"

31 And he said to him,
"Son, you are always with me,
and all that is mine is yours.

32 It was fitting to make merry and be glad,
for this your brother was dead, and he is alive;
he was lost, and is found".'

§241. THE UNJUST STEWARD

            Lk 16:1-9

1 He also said to the disciples,
'There was a rich man who had a steward,
and charges were brought against him that this man was wasting his goods.

2 And he called him and said to him,
"What is this that I hear about you?
Turn in the account of your stewardship, for you can no longer be steward."

3 And the steward said to himself,
"What shall I do, since my master is taking the stewardship away from me?
I am not strong enough to dig, and I am ashamed to beg.

4 I have decided what to do,
so that people may receive me into their houses
when I am put out of the stewardship."

5 So, summoning his master's debtors one by one, he said to the first,
"How much do you owe my master?"

6 He said, "A hundred measures of oil."
And he said to him,
"Take your bill, and sit down quickly and write fifty."

7 Then he said to another,
"And how much do you owe?"
He said, "A hundred measures of wheat."
He said to him, "Take your bill, and write eighty."

8 The master commended the dishonest steward for his shrewdness;
for the sons of the world are more shrewd in dealing with their
own generation
than the sons of light.

9 And I tell you,
make friends for yourselves by means of unrighteous mammon,
so that when it fails
they may receive you into the eternal habitations.' ≤

What it's all about

There are many ancient Church witnesses to the origin of the synoptic gospels. The oldest testimony come from a certain *Papias*, who was bishop of Hierapolis in Asia Minor around 130 when he wrote a book about the words and deeds of Jesus and his disciples. This book has been lost but a number of quotations from it are preserved in the famous *Historia Ecclesiastica* by Eusebius of Caesarea, who lived in the first half of the fourth century. Beside Papias we find many witnesses in the writings of the Church Fathers and also in other texts from the second and third centuries. These witnesses from the ancient Church gave shape to what became the traditional view about the origin of the synoptic gospels. On the whole we get the following picture.

– *Matthew*, the tax collector, one of the twelve apostles (see Mt 9:9; 10:3), was the first one to write a gospel. He wrote it in Palestine for Christians converted from Judaism. His work, written in the 'Hebrew language' (by which they in fact meant Aramaic) was later translated into Greek. The original is lost, the Greek translation is the present gospel of Matthew.

– John *Mark*, a disciple of the apostles from Jerusalem (Acts 12:12) who had first helped Paul in his apostolate (Acts 12:25; 13:5,13; Philem 24; 2 Tim 4:11), and then his cousin Barnabas (Acts 15:37,39; Col 4:10) and finally Peter (1 Pet 5:13) for whom he acted as translator, wrote down in Rome Peter's oral catechesis.

– *Luke*, another disciple, a doctor (Col 4:14), was, unlike the first two, of gentile origin (Col 4:10-14), some say from Antioch in Syria. He travelled with Paul on his second and third missions (Acts 16:10ff; 20:5ff) and also accompanied Paul during his two periods of imprisonment in Rome (Acts 27-28; 2 Tim 4:11) and was the third one to write a gospel. This gospel relies on Paul's apostolic authority as Mark relies on Peter's, while Matthew was himself a witness to Jesus' public life. Luke also wrote a second book, Acts of the Apostles. According to tradition, the gospels of Mark and Luke differ from Matthew in that they were originally written in Greek.

Of course, the ancient ecclesiastical witnesses are important for studying the gospels. The problem of what is called the 'Aramaic Matthew' is still not definitively solved. Modern exegesis takes into consideration the possibility of an Aramaic 'proto-gospel' – but, of course, the present gospel of Matthew is no longer thought to be an exact translation of it. The traditional view that Mark reflects Peter's preaching also plays a certain role in modern biblical research. But there are now well-founded reasons (see below) for no longer accepting the ancient witnesses unquestioningly as the explanation of how the gospels came to be. Even in antiquity these witnesses were disputed. Eusebius is rather severe in judging Papias' credibility. In the first place, there is the problem presented by the ancient witnesses themselves. To what degree are they independent of one another? What sources did *they* use? To what degree are they representative of an accurate historical tradition reaching back to the years 60-100 or even earlier? To what degree have these ancient authors, when sufficient documentation was not at hand, not themselves drawn inferences on the basis of reasonings, conclusions, associations and comparisons? To what degree have pseudepigraphical or apologetic motives played a role? In the second place – and this is more important – the gospels demonstrate a number of characteristics and cause a number of problems to arise which cannot be solved merely by using the external witnesses from ancient Church texts, but only through *internal criticism.* We may state that the ancient tradition on the origin of the gospels has been superseded by the irrefutable data of internal criticism.

In the course of modern gospel research it has gradually become evident that the question of the origin of the gospels for the most part coincides with the question of their interrelationship. In the traditional explanation the question of their interrelationship played no special role. This had to do with the idea of the Holy Spirit's inspiration, whose working was, as we saw, thought to be strongly 'mechanical' (intervening, correcting, replacing) and independent of human channels. It was thought that the evangelists certainly did not need one another to create their works, and that the texts came into being independently.

Matthew and John had written eye-witness accounts while Mark reflected Peter's recollections and Luke, Paul's preaching which was seen as of equal to that of the other apostles. Moreover, for the infancy narratives, Matthew and Luke refer back to Mary and to Joseph's family. Of course, even in antiquity it was noted that there were discrepancies and contradictions in the texts. In general these difficulties were solved by interpreting the texts in a 'mystical sense' (*sensus mysticus*, e.g. by Augustine) or in an 'allegorical sense' (*sensus allegoricus*, e.g. by Origen). But the method of 'harmonizing the gospels', of which we spoke earlier, was by far the most frequently used. This harmonized reading, which dominated catechesis, devotion and liturgy for centuries, was so influential that many believers are even now unable to see the real difficulties in the gospel texts because they are used to reading everything from the *a priori* position of the gospel harmonization. For a long time the Church trembled at the thought of a synopsis, because this put the spotlight on the indefensibility of the harmonization procedure. The different forms of biblical criticism, developed in modern times (text criticism, literary criticism, historical criticism, etc.) had already long before demonstrated convincingly just how much the gospels in their editing and transmission have been subject to the same rules as *all other* types of literary tradition. This insight had consequences for presenting anew the question of how the gospels came to be.

The special relationship of the two 'teams' of evangelists – if the first three, independent of one another, had written a gospel that was so similar to the others, why was the fourth one then so different? – led to the question of the gospel's independence. The more, from the eighteenth century onward, they were read synoptically, the more attention was given to aspects in the gospel texts which formerly had been ignored. The 'new' problems had especially to do with little details which were inconsequential for preaching, catechesis and liturgy and therefore received no attention in these contexts. But some details in the texts were so alienating, that the question of the gospel's mutual relationship became ever more insistent. *The question of the gospels' origin was for the most part identical with the question of their interrelationship*. The synoptic problem or 'synoptic question' was born.

The history of synoptic research is one of slow and painfully careful searching. The matter was (and is) indeed delicate because it is closely related to views on inspiration, inerrancy (infallibility), historicity, authenticity, and truth. Theological interpretation of the Scriptures and synoptic research could not leave one another untouched. A lot of water passed under the bridge before it was recognized that a synoptic reading of the gospels posed no danger to the faith, but rather could lead to an ever deeper and better understanding of their real purpose and message.

The synoptic problem, the facts

The noteworthy relationship between the gospels of Matthew, Mark and Luke has two aspects. On the one hand we see that a striking *agreement* exists among the three in terms of the *material* they contain, the *ordering* of this material and the choice of their *forms of expression* and *vocabulary*. On the other hand, we note a number of *differences* which, precisely because of the numerous agreements, are very surprising. The question has to be put that if all three so closely resemble one another to the point of very details (see below), why are they not completely identical. Looking at it from the perspective of the differences, we suddenly find agreements in places where they are not expected, and conversely, looking at it from the perspective of the agreements, the differences are equally unexpected. Exegesis has long spoken of a *concordia discors*, a discordant concordance.

We will examine the main elements of the problem using a few clear examples.

Agreements and differences in substance or content

The note in Jn 20:30, 'Now Jesus did many other signs in the presence of the disciples, which are not written in this book', is also true of the synoptic gospels. The gospels offer only a choice, a selection from all what Jesus said and did. To the question, 'How is it that they generally seem to have made the same selection?', we could answer, 'Because it just happened that way. The evangelists give an ordered eye-witness report of events using their own recollections or those of the apostles.' But then the problems would really pile up, for the so remarkable difference with John becomes incomprehensible. Either the eye-witness reports of the first three reflects the reality and is John's ordering wrong, or else the four evangelists, independent of one another, make a selection from what they have seen and heard, in which case it is incomprehensible that three so closely resemble one another while the fourth plays 'lone ranger'. Referring back to the 'inspiration of the Holy Spirit' can at best function as a *deus ex machina* – why should three be inspired to so similar a version while the fourth is inspired to such a totally different version? In other words, why are the similarities and differences not equally divided over all four gospels?

The problem does not become any easier when we come up against the differences within the synoptic gospels. To form a picture of these differences that has a certain degree of clarity, it is useful to have a short overview of the gospel's *material* – i.e. in terms of the content, the text matter.

≥ – The elements (here exegesis speaks of 'textual units' or *pericopes*, distinguishable pieces of text which form a whole of themselves) which Matthew, Mark and Luke have in common are called the *triple tradition* (or *triple matter*). A few examples: Mt 9:1-17 // Mk 2:1-22 // Lk 5:17-29 (see above, p. 86); Mt 26:30-58 // Mk 14:26-54 // Lk 22:39-55 (// means parallel text, parallel pericope).

– Many texts are also common to Matthew and Luke but are *not* found in Mark. These are mainly words or discourses of Jesus. In this case we speak of the *double tradition*. Note that the term *double tradition* is only applicable to pericopes which Matthew and Luke have in common, not to texts which Matthew *or* Luke have in common with Mark (but not with each other). A few examples: Mt 4:2-11 // Lk 4:2b-13 (see above p. 87); Mt 5:3-12 // Lk 6:20b-23; Mt 6:25-34 // Lk 12:22-31.

– Finally there is also the *single tradition*. As the name says, it has to do with material present in only one of the gospels, material having no parallels in the others. It is customary to use here the German technical term *Sondergut* (literally, special material) abbreviated SgMt, SgMk, SgLk. Some examples: Mt 6:1-8,16-18 (see above, p. 90); 11:28-30; 18:23-35; Mk 4:26-29; Lk 10:29-37; 15:8-32 (see above, p. 91); 24:13-49. ≤

Mark has nearly no *Sondergut*. This means that the material in Mark's gospel is nearly integrally included in Matthew and/or Luke. Put differently, nearly the whole of Mark (with but few exceptions) belongs to the triple tradition. Approximately 22% of Matthew's gospel and 20% of Luke's share material having no parallel in Mark. This is the part we call the 'double tradition'. 28% of Matthew's gospel is *Sondergut* (SgMt), while Luke has 41% *Sondergut* (SgLk). Luke has thus by far the largest proportion of *Sondergut*.

Seen schematically, the material is divided as follows:

	Matthew	Mark	Luke
Total number of verses	1070	660	1150
Triple tradition	537 // Mk	630 // Mt-Lk	442 // Mk
Double Tradition	234 // Lk	–	229 // Mt
Sondergut	299 SgMt	30 SgMk	479 SgLk

It is obvious that in a good synopsis one can immediately see whether a given pericope belongs to the triple, double or single tradition.[2] It is, of course, the task of biblical research to explain as well as possible these agreements and differences in the gospel's text material.

Agreements and differences in the ordering of the content

The question of the agreements and differences in the *ordering* has been shown to be of particular importance in studying the internal relationships among the three gospels. Here, too, we are confronted with surprising observations.

– The equivalency in the ordering (the exegetical term for the ordering of pericopes is *acolouthon*) within the *triple tradition* is remarkable. With but few exceptions, the material common to Matthew, Mark and Luke is ordered in the same way. This means that we meet the same pericopes in the three evangelists in the same positions in the course of their gospels (e.g. Mt 9:1-17 // Mk 2:1-22 // Lk 5:17-39 – see above p. 84 ff – following the same acolouthon: healing of a palsied man, the call of Levi, Jesus eats with tax collectors and sinners, the question about fasting and the old and the new). The same ordering of the triple material leads to the similarity in shape of the general chronological and geographical framework of Jesus' life in the three gospels. Jesus' activity in all three follows roughly the same four-part schema:

	Matthew	Mark	Luke
1. Preparing the mission	3:1-4:11	1:1-13	3:1-4:13
2. Mission in Galilee	4:12-18:35	1:14-9:50	4:14-9-50
3. Progress toward Jerusalem	19:10-20:34	10:1-52	9:51-19:27
4. Passion and resurrection	21-28	11-16	19:28-14

We could make the remark that the equivalent ordering is obvious, since that is what happened in Jesus' public life! The ordering has to be the same in all three! But then we are again left with the problem of John. In John the events are clearly arranged in a *different ordering*. There, Jesus comes at least three time to Jerusalem; the cleansing of the temple takes place at the beginning of his mission, etc.

There is more. Within the general similarity in the acolouthon of the synoptic events, surprising differences do often arise. As soon as we become aware of this, we can no longer claim for the synoptic authors an equivalent ordering with the supposition that it is so similar because everything happened in that way. Even within the synoptics the order of the material is only partly the same.

We illustrate what we mean with three examples.

≥ – The healing of Peter's mother-in-law, Mt 8:14-15 // Mk 1:29-31 // Lk 4:38-39. Matthew and Mark tell of the healing of Peter's mother-in-law *after* the calling of the first disciples and Luke *before* (see Mt 4:18-22 // Mk 1:16-20 // Lk 5:1-11). Noteworthy is that Luke does agree with Mark in situating the healing at a moment when Jesus is coming out of the synagogue in Capernaum, while Matthew does not do this, but has the healing of Peter's mother-in-law preceded by the healing of a leper which in Mark comes *after* the healing of Peter's mother-in-law and which in Luke comes immediately after the calling of the disciples.

– Oddly enough, in between the healing of the leper and the healing of Peter's mother-in-law, Matthew mentions the healing of the centurion's servant (Mt 8:5-13), which in Luke is told in chapter 7 verses 1-10. If we remove the pericope of the healing of the leper from Matthew, we see then that his version of the healing of the centurion's son follows the same words of Jesus as they do in Luke, namely, the saying on the poorly built house (Mt 7:24-27 // Lk 6:47-49). These word form the conclusion of one of Jesus' discourses which we find in both Matthew and Luke (in Matthew it is called the 'sermon on the mount'; in Luke the 'sermon on the plain'). The place of this discourse in the chronological framework of Jesus' mission again does not agree. In Matthew it is Jesus' great 'action plan' (J. Lambrecht) for everything else that is told of Jesus' deeds. In Luke, Jesus had already done a great deal before the discourse. These difficulties cannot be solved by saying that Matthew does not mention the deeds that took place before the sermon on the mount, for the events we just looked at *are* the events which Luke puts before the sermon on the plain, i.e. Matthew puts after the sermon what Luke puts before. Nor can we solve it by saying Jesus gave the same discourse twice, once in an extended version before his deed in Capernaum and a shorter version afterward and that Matthew and Luke each gave a different version so they would not have to repeat one another. This presupposes they knew of one another's gospels – which, as will see, is highly unlikely. But it does not explain why they elsewhere reflect identical words and events. Matthew's sermon on the mount and Luke's sermon on the plain are fundamentally the same tradition of Jesus sayings, but put in a different place in the gospel (see below on the ordering in the double tradition).

– We see something similar in connection with the Lord's Prayer. In Matthew, the Lord's Prayer is the centre piece of the sermon on the mount, Mt 6:9-15. In Luke, Jesus teaches his disciples the Lord's Prayer in a completely different context, namely, while travelling to Jerusalem, Lk 11:1-4. But oddly enough, Luke immediately follows the Lord's Prayer with a question on petitionary prayer which we find in Matthew also in the sermon on the mount. Compare Lk 11:9-13 with Mt 7:7-11. ≤

We meet such problems frequently. They illustrate abundantly that we cannot reconstruct an exact chronology of the facts and words. There is in the acolouthon a discordant concordance.

– Of the examples above, the last two belong to the *double tradition*. In the double tradition there are also several remarkable things to note on the order of the pericopes. When we look at the pericopes common to Matthew and Luke within the whole of the gospel, we notice that many of these identical texts come in other places in their gospels. We already referred to the sermons on the mount and plain, the Lord's Prayer and the question on petitionary prayer. Compare also Mt 6:25-34 with Lk 12:22-31. Such examples are numerous. Yet when we look at the matter more deeply, we come upon the astonishing fact that when we lift the double tradition out of the whole of the two gospels and look at it separately – i.e. we put aside all what belongs to the triple tradition and *Sondergut* and put the texts of the double tradition side by side – we see that there is a strikingly equivalent ordering in Matthew and Luke.

This is an extremely conspicuous fact that has intrigued exegetes greatly and has contributed to the solution of the synoptic problem. We receive the impression that Matthew and Luke have used a more or less similar basic text for their double tradition, but that they pulled it apart and inserted the pieces in different places within the framework of their gospels. In saying this we are anticipating somewhat the solutions to the synoptic question, but the peculiar discordant concordance of the double tradition gradually allows us to suspect that a solution to some of the problems around these gospels should be sought in the evangelist's editorial work.

≥ To illustrate the peculiar phenomenon of the ordering in the double tradition, we include a table from the Denaux-Vervenne synopsis which contains the main elements of the double tradition in a systematic classification. The first column contains references to Luke, the third to Matthew. The middle column contains the 'titles' of the various elements.

Luke			Matthew
1.	3:7-9.16-17	John's preaching of repentance	3:7-12
2.	4:2-13	The temptation	4:2-11
3.	6:20-23.27-30. (31).23-36	The sermon on the mount	5:3-6.11-12. 39-42 (7:12)
4.	6:37-38.41-49	The sermon on the plain	7:1-5.16-21.24-27
5.	7:1-10	The centurion's servant	8:5-10.13
6.	7:18-35	Sayings on John the Baptist	11:2-19
7.	10:13-15	Woes on the cities of Galilee	11:21-23
8.	10:21-22	Christ's thanksgiving to the Father	11:25-26
9.	11:14-23	The Pharisees' accusation	12:22-30
10.	11:24-26	The return of the evil spirit	12:43-45
11.	11:39-52	Woes against the Pharisees	23:4.23-25.29-36
12.	13:34-35	The lament over Jerusalem	23:37-39
13.	17:23-27.34-37	The day of the Son of Man	24:26-28.37-41
14.	19:12-27	The parable of the talents	25:14-30

Note that the pericopes follow in the same sequence in Luke and in Matthew. In both, the centurion's servant comes before the sayings on John the Baptist and this before the woes on the cities of Galilee, etc. The first and third columns of the table show for both references in increasing sequence. But within the whole of their different gospels, many of the elements are found in different places. This is striking for the placing of the sermons on the mount/plain, but even more so for all the pericopes starting with no. 7 in the table. Luke puts pericopes 7 to 14 all in the long journey to Jerusalem, thus *after* Jesus left Galilee and *before* entering the city. But in Matthew pericopes 7 to 10 take place in Galilee and 11 to 14 inside the walls of Jerusalem. This point will be raised again when presenting the solution to the synoptic question, particularly when discussing Lachmann's postulate. ≤

Agreements and differences in forms of expression and choice of words

In this area, too, we meet a peculiar *concordia discors*.
≥ – Let us compare Mt 4:18 with Mk 1:16 and note the addition, 'for they were fishermen'; or Mt 24:15 with Mk 13:14 and the addition, 'Let the reader understand' precisely in the same place in Jesus' discourses. Yet this cannot be something Jesus himself said at the time, since it is the evangelist who addresses readers (let the *reader* understand). Compare also Mt 9:6 with Mk 2:10 and Lk 5:24 where in all three Jesus' answer to the scribes is interrupted in the same way with the expression, '– and then he said to the paralytic –'. The same is true for the description of Judas as 'one of the twelve' in Mt 26:47 // Mk 14:43 // Lk 22:47. Why must Matthew and Mark and Luke explain precisely in the same place that Judas was one of the twelve? In all these (and many similar) cases it is a question of precise agreements in detail which we would not normally expect from people relating a story independently of one another – certainly not with the frequency with which they occur in the gospels. It is just such detailed agreements which make readers of texts other than the gospels think of literal quotations from someone else's work.

 – We meet a similar phenomenon in terms of *word choice*. In the temptation story we are told how Jesus was brought to the pinnacle of the temple. Matthew and Luke both use here the Greek word *pterugion* (Mt 4:5 // Lk 4:9). In the whole of Greek literature this work is used *only here* with this meaning! Even stronger is the example from the Lord's Prayer. There we read the word *epiausios*, which we render in our prayer text as *daily* bread (Mt 6:11 // Lk 11:13). This word is found nowhere else in Greek literature in any sense at all, and its translation cannot be determined with certainty. Can we easily imagine that two independent authors presenting the Lord's Prayer should agree in such rare words or (for the pinnacle of the temple) in such rare meanings of words? Remember that we cannot solve this problem by saying that the word comes from Jesus himself, since Jesus did not teach the Lord's Prayer in Greek but in Aramaic and there are many more normal and understandable Greek translations for the word 'daily'.

– But at the same time there are always startling differences. While we meet the most unexpected, striking agreements in words and expressions which are in fact not so very important (such as the pinnacle of the temple or '– and then he said to the paralytic –'), we find differences in words which are theologically much more important and in places where we would least expect them. We think here in particular of the words over the bread and wine at the last supper which we would normally expect to be deeply engraved in memory, but which are not exactly the same in any of the gospels (Mt 26:26-29 // Mk 14:22-25 // Lk 22:15-20; even the oldest known version of these words in 1 Cor 11:23f contains another variant). The sign above the cross differs somewhat among the various evangelists, even though this was a written text! Compare Mt 37:37 with Mk 15:26, Lk 23:38 and also Jn 19:19. ≤

The highly simplified overview given above can give some idea of the problems which exegesis of the synoptics faces. If the evangelists were 'inspired' to such strikingly similar forms of speech and choice of words in such unimportant texts, how can we explain the conspicuous differences in texts which seem so much more important? If they had worked independently how do we explain their concordance – since John does not share it? And if they did have contact with one another, why is this concordance so discordant?

The synoptic problem, in search of a solution

It can be imagined how carefully the way to an answer has been explored. The history of synoptic research is one of the study of details in the most literal sense of the term, every word every syllable is examined and discussed from all directions.

It is often just the most 'conspicuous' details that have set exegesis on the right trail. The history of the synoptic tradition has been one of many attempts and failures, many theories and corrections, but also one of brilliant results. Here we can only present the highlights of this unusually fascinating investigation.

Various attempts

The starting point of modern synoptic insights is the conviction shared by all exegetes – and based on the problems of *concordia discors* which we have described above – that the peculiar relationship among the gospels of Matthew, Mark and Luke can only be explained when we accept that, in some way or other, a connection existed among the three of them. What connection? This is exactly what examination was to show.

By the end of the eighteenth century a solution was being sought from two directions: (1) In one, the connection among the synoptics was explained as follows: the evangelists wrote their gospels independently of one another but followed the same models. Within this direction there developed various *model* or *example* theories. (2) In the other, the evangelists did *not* work independently of one another but in one way or another used one another's texts. This direction led to a variety of *use theories*.

1. Within the *model theories* various directions were possible. They were often defended with great scholarship and much energy, but none was completely satisfactory. The one theory arose as a correction to another. Some authors thought the evangelists had used a now lost gospel or *proto-gospel* (e.g. G.E. Lessing, J.G. Eichhorn). We could think here of the Aramaic version of Matthew that we mentioned above (see p. 66). The theory of a proto-gospel was abandoned because it met too many unsolvable problems, but elements from the theory still have a place in modern gospel research (cf chapter 3, n. 7). Other authors did not presuppose a written proto-gospel but

rather a *shared oral tradition* which was already firmly crystallized (e.g. J.G. Herder, J. Gieseler and D.F. Strauss). These theories were also only partly satisfactory, in particular because they could not fully explain the difference in the ordering of the details. Still others, such as F. Schleiermacher, suggested that the evangelists used several fragmentary sources. Using a word in the prologue to Luke's gospel, exegetes called these sources *diegese* and we speak of a *fragment* or *diegese theory*.[3]

One defender of the fragment theory, the classics scholar Karl Lachmann, made an ingenious discovery in 1835. He had taken the triple tradition aside and studied it thoroughly and came to a startling conclusion with regard to the ordering of the pericopes. (Note well, here it is important to remember that the reasoning has to do with *the ordering of the pericopes in the triple tradition, i.e. the tradition the three gospels have in common.* We have to imagine someone putting this material in three columns side by side and comparing the order of the individual text units.) Lachmann noticed that there was a rather serious difference in the ordering of the pericopes when looking at the whole of Matthew, Mark and Luke, or even when looking at the whole of Matthew and Luke, but that the difference in ordering was much smaller when comparing Matthew with Mark or Luke with Mark. In other words, the agreement in the order of the stories is great between Matthew and Mark and is even greater between Luke and Mark (Luke has, in fact, only five important cases of reordering when compared to Mark). However, when we put the three gospels side by side the difference is, as we said, noticeably greater. In this way Lachmann discovered that the greater difference in order noticed when we put the three gospels side by side, or when comparing Matthew with Luke, comes from the fact that Matthew and Luke each differ from Mark's order in different places.

Lachmann also saw that Matthew and Luke agree on the ordering of the stories *only there where they also agree with Mark.* In the ordering of the triple tradition, Matthew and Luke *never* agree with one another against Mark. Where they differ from on another, one of them has always kept Mark's ordering. This allowed Lachmann to conclude that *in Mark we find the main source for the ordering of the triple tradition* and that Matthew and Luke's differences with one another can be explained by the fact that *one of them had in each case changed the order found in Mark's gospel.* Moreover, Lachmann had taken into consideration that Matthew and Luke had inserted the material from the *double tradition in different places* in their gospels. (See the table above, p. 103). This strengthened the German scholar's conviction that we have to look for the basic material and the basic ordering of the synoptic gospels in Mark's gospel to which Matthew and Luke had each independently added other material. This meant that for Lachmann the triple tradition, found as a whole in Mark, was older than and had precedence over the other material found in the gospels of Matthew and Luke. All this led Lachmann to formulate his famous *postulate: in the triple tradition, Mark has the intermediary position.* The re-discovery of the wheel? In any case, a discovery of capital importance for the further study of the synoptic gospels!

According to Lachmann, this meant that a common text lay at the basis of the synoptic gospels, a text containing five fragments (*diegese;* Lachmann called them 'corpuscula') whose order Mark had fully respected while Matthew and Luke had made changes. This final conclusion would not survive, but his postulate was a giant step in the direction of a satisfactory answer. But this would only be reached several years later when Lachmann's postulate was connected with the use theory.

2. The *use theory*, as we said, is based on the conviction that the evangelists had, in some way or other, used one another's texts. The question here is, of course, who used whom? Here too many different directions are possible. When we accept that Matthew was the first gospel and was used by the others, then we speak of *Matthean priority*. Since Matthew was unanimously considered by tradition to be the first gospel, this theory was long dominant and even today has its defenders (especially via the detour of the Aramaic Matthew). Those who think Luke is the first evangelist speak of *Lucan priority. Marcan priority*, suggested for the first time in 1786 by C. Storr, was for a time

not taken seriously. Mark was traditionally looked upon as the little brother of the two 'major gospels'. There was even a theory which claimed that Mark had made a summary of the larger gospels.

Lachmann's discovery would turn the tide. Lachmann himself did not think that Matthew or Luke made direct use of Mark (see above), but his *postulate had made Mark the basis of the agreement among the three gospels*. Once this view entered the use theory the road was made free for Marcan priority. In 1838 C.G. Wilke defended Marcan priority with 'German thoroughness'. But a month before Wilke's important study, a philosopher from Leipzig, Christian Hermann Weisse, published a two-volume work entitled *Die Evangelische Geschichte, kritisch und philologisch bearbeitet* [*The history of the gospels, critically and philologically considered*]. Here he developed a hypothesis which has become known as the *two-source theory* and which is the leading model for modern exegesis of the synoptic gospels. Its definitive breakthrough is a result of the profound arguments presented in its favour by H.J. Holzmann in 1863.[4]

The two-source theory

At the basis of the two-source theory lies the conviction that the common 'model' for the synoptics must not be sought outside the gospels but within them, i.e. the use theory. The second step came when it was realized that Mark and not Matthew or Luke lies at the basis of the agreements among the three. In other words, the gospel of Mark was itself the model for the other two. Mark is the *source* of Matthew and Luke. That is how Weisse explained the triple tradition. But an explanation for the double tradition had to be sought elsewhere; since Mark does not contain material from the double tradition, it cannot serve as the source of this material for Matthew and Luke. For the double tradition Weisse will develop a type of model theory which explains the agreements between Matthew and Luke.

We present now the whole of the two-source theory as follows:

– Matthew and Luke each independently used Mark's gospel in composing their own gospels. Mark is therefore the basis, the *source*, of the triple tradition. Mark is the first source in the two-source theory.

– Matthew and Luke have moreover each independently used sayings or words (= *logia* in Greek) of Jesus. This collection of words or sayings is referred to by the Letter Q (the first letter of the German word *Quelle*, also called *Logienquelle*, see above p. 66). This Quelle is the basis, the *source*, of the double tradition. Q is the second source of the two-source theory.

Note well that the *Quelle theory* grew from the evidence we examined above (p. 66 f), namely, the remarkable fact that most of the pericopes of the double tradition are put in *different places* in Matthew and Luke within the whole of their gospels, but that when they are removed from the framework of the triple tradition they follow *in the same order*. The best explanation for this seems for the time being to be that Matthew and Luke had the same text as model – perhaps in slightly differing copies – whose order they respected for the most part but which they divided into pieces which they inserted independently of one another into different places in their basic gospels. That this source consists primarily in words of Jesus is not a problem. It has been proven since 1945 that such collections did indeed exist. In that year, in the Egyptian village of Nag-Hammadi, a collection of Coptic manuscripts was found (51 texts in 13 codices) dating from the fourth and fifth centuries. One of them is the famous gnostic gospel of Thomas which most likely goes back to a Syrian original dating from the middle of the second century and containing nothing other than 114 'sayings of Jesus' some of which may go back to the first century. It was published for the first time in 1959.

– Matthew and Luke have also each their *Sondergut* from elsewhere, partly from sources no longer confidently ascertainable. Here there is also a question of the evangelists' own creative contribution. On this point there is no consensus among exegetes.

Diagram of the two-source theory

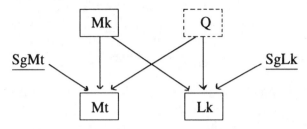

Using this diagram we can summarize (in simplified fashion) the two-source theory as follows:

Mark wrote the first real and complete gospel. His work is the basis of the general form and general framework of the synoptic gospels. He is responsible for the arrangement of the triple tradition material within the gospels.

When *Matthew* and *Luke* edited their gospels they used the exiting gospel of Mark already circulating in their communities. We may assume quite concretely that when preparing their texts (slightly varying?) copies of Mark's gospel lay on their desks and that they borrowed from it their basic material and general framework. Moreover, Matthew and Luke each had a copy of another written document, the collection of sayings or *Quelle* which may have been used within their communities as a handbook for preaching and catechesis. They each – independently of the other – took the sayings of Jesus which tradition had gathered together (most likely still in Palestine) and inserted them in Mark's basic text in places where they thought best fit with the events and where it best served their theological picture of Jesus. Since Matthew and Luke each had their own style and each wanted to place their own theological accents on their work *neither just copied Mark and the Quelle literally* but changed the place of some passages, and adapted and corrected others. It is even possible that their copies of Mark were not absolutely identical nor their copies of the *Quelle*. This explains why F. Neirynck was able to publish a synopsis of the *Quelle* in 1988 – a Q-synopsis. As it should have become clear from the chapter on the development of the evangelical tradition, the *Quelle* is older than Mark (see above p. 66). Modern exegesis is still studying the question of whether Mark did not possibly know of the *Quelle*. Opinions on this are divided. Should it turn out that this question is answered positively, it still remains very difficult to explain why he did not make full use of it. That is why many people think he did not know it, at least not in this form.

It is important now to draw immediate attention to the conclusion to which the two-source theory leads, a conclusion which is very important for the interpretation of the gospels. *Neither Matthew's nor Luke's gospel gives a direct and first-hand eye-witness account*, since they are based on two existing sources, namely, Mark's gospel and the collection of Jesus' sayings. The differences among the synoptic gospels must therefore, as a rule, not be attributed to 'other recollections' (of eye-witnesses) but to the evangelists' editorial intervention. The motives for this intervention have primarily a structural, stylistic and theological character.

In addition to the two sources, Matthew and Luke have much *Sondergut*. In Luke it concerns a large part of his best known texts: the good Samaritan, Zacchaeus, the prodigal son, Lazarus and the rich man, the travellers to Emmaus, etc. As we said the precise origin of this material can no longer be discovered. It must come largely from the oral Jesus traditions in the evangelists' own communities. Perhaps it also partly goes back to smaller written sources available to only one of the evangelists. Perhaps a small part of the *Sondergut* belonged to the *Quelle*, *Quelle* material preserved by only one of the evangelists. There can also be (especially in Luke) strong editorial contributions from the evangelists. Whoever is familiar with John's way of working is no longer surprised that this is also possible in the synoptic authors.

In this regard one more important thing remains to be said, the infancy narratives in Matthew and Luke do not belong – as we could expect – to the double tradition but to the *Sondergut*.

A. Denaux and M. Vervenne summarize the importance of the two-source theory in the introduction to their synopsis as follows:

The great advantage of the two-source theory is that it offers the simplest solution for the whole body of literary peculiarities which study of the synoptic gospels has brought to light. The agreements and differences in material, ordering and vocabulary are explained without artificiality. The material common to both Matthew and Luke is derived from Mark and Q; Matthew and Luke's ordering, or acolouthon, comes from the dominant role played by the 'proto-gospel' Mark into whose ordering Matthew and Luke inserted and integrated the Q-material, each according to his interest and intention; agreements and differences in vocabulary are due to Matthew and Luke each more or less freely and independently using their sources Mark and Q (*op. cit.*, p. XLII).

Even for other problems (doublets in the gospels – see below p. 114 – the presence of theology typical of Mark in Matthew and Luke but not the reverse, etc.) the two-source theory still offers the best solution. Some questions are as yet not fully answered, but the theory is being polished further every day.[5]

One thing must remain clear, i.e. the two-source theory is not an unquestionably proven matter like the shape of the earth. Its scientific status remains that of a hypothesis. But this does not justify the conclusion that any and every other hypothesis is of equal value. An hypothesis is not the same thing as caprice or fantasy. Since 1863 the two-source theory has proven itself to be the best work hypothesis for the story of the synoptic gospels and has since then been confirmed by an ever increasing number of results. The results of form criticism and tradition criticism have not undermined it, on the contrary, they have supported it. It is a little like the theory of evolution. The scientific status of the teaching about evolution is also still that of a hypothesis, and there are many questions for which it has as yet no solution; the theory of evolution must also be continually polished and corrected. But this does not justify the conclusion that we may continue to assert that the world was created in six days or (in agreement with biblical chronology) that it is less than 6000 years old.

≥ Finally we will give two examples to illustrate the way the synoptic authors worked.

1. We compare Mt 8:18-22 with Lk 9:57-60.

Mt 8:18-22	Lk 9:57-60
18 Now when Jesus saw great crowds around him, he gave orders to go over to the other side.	
	57 And they were going along the road, a man said to him, 'I will follow you wherever you go.'
19 And a scribe came up and said to him, 'Teacher, I will follow you wherever you go.'	
20 And Jesus said to him, 'Foxes have holes, and birds of the air have nests; but the son of man has nowhere to lay his head.'	58 And Jesus said to him, 'Foxes have holes, and birds of the air have nests; but the son of man has nowhere to lay his head.'
21 Another of the disciples said to him,	59 To another he said, 'Follow me.' But he said, 'Lord, let me first go to bury my father.'
'Lord, let me first go and bury my father.'	
22 But Jesus said to him, 'Follow me, and leave the dead to bury their own dead.'	60 But he said to him, 'Leave the dead to bury their own dead; but as for you, go and proclaim the kingdom of God.'

– In both texts the words which Jesus speaks are given in almost literally the same way, but the situation is different. In Matthew the event takes place just as Jesus is about to step into the boat to sail in the crossing where the storm at sea will occur. In Luke it takes place on the way to Jerusalem.

– Luke also tells the story of the storm at sea (Lk 8:22-35), and Matthew also tells the story of the journey to Jerusalem. In this they both agree with Mark; thus this material comes from the triple tradition. But Luke does *not* recount Jesus' sayings (on the foxes and birds and on burying the dead) at the time of the storm at sea, while Matthew does *not* recount them during the journey to Jerusalem. The best explanation for this situation lies in accepting that we have here in Matthew and Luke the same Jesus-words preserved by tradition but included in their gospels in different places.

– These Jesus-words are present in Matthew and Luke but *not* in Mark. Thus they belong to the double tradition. The words are almost literally the same, but the stories around them are different. Luke is very vague about who is involved ('a man' in v. 57; 'another' in v. 59). Matthew is more precise ('a scribe' in v. 19; 'another of his disciples' in v. 21). Verse 59 in Luke is more of a short call story where Jesus himself takes the initiative with 'Follow me'; in Matthew verse 21 is not a call story, yet remarkably we find Jesus' words 'follow me' in verse 22. This leads us to suspect strongly that Matthew and Luke both worked on the basis of a source containing these words of Jesus, but having no precise identification of the people involved, the location or the situation in which they were spoken. A source containing mainly Jesus' *words* means – in the light of what we learned above – the *Quelle*. The fact that this source consists almost solely of Jesus' words gave the evangelists great freedom in placing the words in their gospels and in determining their narrative framework, although differences in the copies of Q in circulation could also have an influence here. On the whole, the evangelists remain very faithful to the words themselves.

– *Matthew* puts Jesus' saying on following in the framework of the storm at sea. The words are put between the order to get in the boat (8:18) and the sailing to the other side (8:23ff). In doing so Matthew gives the words a profound dimension. In his eyes, following Jesus means remaining faithful to his call, even when storm and problems arise, in the full faith that Christ is ultimately the saving Lord, even from storms! And this message was very important for a community like Matthew's which had to face so much opposition.

– *Luke*, on the other hand, puts the same sayings of Jesus at the beginning of the journey to Jerusalem. He puts the scene between the comment that Jesus sent messengers ahead of him (9:51) and the appointment of 70 disciples to go out and preach (10:1). In this context the small addition is conspicuous: 'Go and proclaim the kingdom of God.' For Luke following Christ means in the first place following Jesus on his way to Jerusalem, the place where the promises of salvation will be filled through suffering and death, and preaching God's kingdom along the way.

This shows how enriching the parallel reading of the gospels can be. The way Matthew and Luke place Jesus' words reveals their specific theological accents. Each highlights a fundamental aspect of following. For Matthew it is loyalty to the faith in difficult circumstances. For Luke it is the proclaiming of God's kingdom, even if this proclaiming 'leads to Jerusalem' where the cross awaits. Using this 'same' text we could easily write two different and complementary homilies on the meaning of following Jesus depending on whether we used Matthew's or Luke's context.

2. We compare Mt 12:38-42 with Lk 11:29-32

Mt 12:38-42	Lk 11:29-32
38 Some of the scribes and Pharisees said to him, 'Teacher, we wish to see a sign from you.'	29 When the crowds were increasing, he began to say
39 But he answered them 'An evil and adulterous generation seeks for a sign; but no sign shall be given to it except for the sign of the prophet Jonah.	'This generaion is an evil generation; it seeks a sign, but no sign shall be given to it except the sign of Jonah.
40 For as Jonah was three days in the belly of the whale, so will the Son of man be three days and three nights in the heart of the earth.	30 For as Jonah became a sign to the men of Nineveh, so will the Son of man be to this generation.
41 The men of Nineveh will arise at the judgement with this generation and condemn it; for they repented at the preaching of Jonah, and behold, something greater than Jonah is here.	32 The men of Nineveh will arise at the judgement with this generation and condemn it; for they repented at the preaching of Jonah, and behold, something greater than Jonah is here.
42 The queen of the South will arise at the judgement with this generation and condemn it; for she came from the ends of the earth to hear the wisdom of Solomon, and behold, soemthing greater than Solomon is here.	31 The queen of the South will arise at the judgement with the men of this generation and condemn them; for she came from the ends of the earth to hear the wisdom of Solomon, and behold, something greater Solomon is here.

Again the framework in which Jesus speaks these words is different in the two gospels. Matthew puts them in the fullness of Jesus' activity in Galilee around the sea. Luke puts them in Jesus' journey to Jerusalem, which starts in chapter 9 verse 51. Notice again the difference in the narrative introduction used by Mt 12:38 and Lk 11:29. Luke's introduction is again more general and Jesus' words are much more unexpected than they are as an answer to a specific question from the scribes and Pharisees found in Matthew. But notice also Lk 11:16 where it says, 'while others, to test him, sought from him a sign from heaven.' For Luke this serves as a long-distance preparation for the sayings in 11:30-32.

– The words, 'no sign shall be given to it *except the sign of Jonah* ,point to a text from the double tradition. Jesus' saying on not giving a sign has also been preserved in the triple tradition; we find it in Mk 8:11-12, but *without* the addition '*except the sign of Jonah*'. Matthew has also preserved the text of the triple tradition (in 16:1-2a,4), even if he does add the words about Jonah. Matthew, therefore, tells twice of a request for a sign and Jesus' answers, once as he found it in Mark and once as he found it in Q. (We call this a doublet; other such doublets also exist and point to the same double origin, i.e. Mark and Q.) Luke gives the story only once.

– Mt 12:40 and Lk 11:30 differ from one another. Luke's text, 'as Jonah became a sign for the men of Nineveh...', seems to fit more logically with verse 32 than Matthew's version, 'For as Jonah was three days and three nights in the belly of the whale ...' which is a quotation from Jon 2:1. The following texts on the men of Nineveh and the Queen of the South are nearly identical, even though in reverse order, where Matthew's order appears more logical. We are dealing here with the double tradition since these texts are not found in Mark. We now have two possibilities. Either the different versions in Mt 12:40 and Lk 11:30 belong to two different versions of the *Quelle*, or else the difference must be sought in the evangelists' own editorial activity in which Matthew follows his custom of using a scriptural quotation to situate Jesus and perhaps for this reason specifies that Jonah is a prophet.

– Regardless, the two versions of this saying of Jesus again highlight each its own aspect of his meaning as 'sign' for the people. For *Luke* the meaning of Jesus' words is that people ask for a sign while not realizing that Jesus himself is the sign. The Ninevites needed only Jonah's words and deeds to be converted. So should Jesus' words and deeds be sufficient in order to hear and be converted without supplementary signs. People not prepared to listen to his words without signs would not believe them anyway. Whoever does not see in Christ himself a sign of God, will certainly not see it in other signs!

– *Matthew* colours Jesus' sign value somewhat differently. He (or perhaps the Q source) has the 'sign of Jonah' refer specifically to Jesus' death and resurrection. As Jonah remained three days in the whale's belly (and was then spat out), so will the Son of man remain three days in the heart (bowels) of the earth (and then arise). This illustrates a very important aspect of Matthew's gospel, namely, all that happened to Jesus is a profound fulfilment of the Scriptures. For him it is clear that people who ask for a sign need only look at Christ's death. *That* is the best of all signs and whoever finds no sign in Christ's passion will certainly find none anywhere else! ≤

This second example also illustrates the richness of parallel reading. Again the editorial 'treatment' of a (perhaps) shorter original Jesus saying has brought to light two important aspects of the gospel message. Whoever desires signs in order to believe must look at Jesus himself. He is the best sign of God's presence among his people as Jonah was for the Ninevites (Luke). Who looks past him to suspend his faith from other signs is missing the whole point. The best example of all is Jesus' passion, cross and resurrection (Matthew). That this has meaning cannot be made any clearer by providing even more signs. It witnesses to itself.

Conclusion to chapter 4

From what we have seen it is clear that the gospels of Matthew, Mark and Luke are more closely related than had been traditionally supposed, since they came to exist in mutual literary dependence. But this by no means says that whoever has read one has read them all! On the contrary, the first three gospels display, in their internal relationships, very individual characteristics revealed in their differences with one another. The same basic picture of Jesus is coloured in an individual way by each of the evangelists. Each of them enriched the traditional picture they received with his own theological accents.

The synoptic gospels can be compared with three children from the same family. Their similar features show they are related to one another, but they each have their own character.

For this reason we will try in the following three chapters to summarize the most important characteristics of the evangelists separately. The unavoidable simplification will undoubtedly not do justice to the richness of the individual gospels, a richness which is to be discovered especially in the small details. The overview sketched here neither can nor intends to be complete or exclusive. It is merely an invitation to give enough attention to the individual character of these so closely related texts when reading the synoptic gospels.

≥ Some exercises relating to the material in this fourth chapter which can be tried in Bible groups are given here.

– Look up the many text references used in this chapter, lay the texts side by side and note particularly well the differences and agreements in the details. They can then be discussed using the information in chapter 4.

– Find other examples of the triple, double and single traditions in the synoptic gospels; look up doublets and compare them; for SgMt and SgLk it is interesting to examine the difference in theme between the two gospels. Matthew's *Sondergut* has a different nature from Luke's. The comparison is a good preparation for studying the singularity of each of the evangelists.

– Look up the texts from the table on p. 103. The difference in the contexts in which they have been placed generally gives the otherwise similar texts a different turn of meaning (see the two examples just discussed). Try to find the differences and discuss them in a group. This is a good exercise for learning to read the gospel texts within their more general context. Note in particular the difference in the narrative introduction or framework of the texts.

It is obvious that a good synopsis will greatly help such study. A really scientific comparison of details is only possible when using the Greek text but for use in English there is H.F.D. Sparks *A Synopsis of the Gospels* (London: Block, 1970-1974). This is a two-volume work whose first volume (now in its second edition) is entitled *The Synoptic Gospels with the Johannine Parallels*. The second volume is *The Gospel According to St John with the Synoptic Parallels*. ≤

NOTES

1　An excellent new synopsis of the first three gospels was published in 1986 for the Dutch language area. It was prepared by the exegetes Adelbert Denaux from Bruges and Mark Vervenne from Leuven. Beside a clear synoptic presentation of the texts, this synopsis also offers a fascinating introduction to the synoptic question. We highly recommend this edition for those who may wish to go deeper into the question. A. Denaux, M. Vervenne, *Synopsis van de eerste drie evangeliën* [*Synopsis of the first three gospels*], Leuven/ Turnhout, VBS/Brepols, 1986, 322 pp. A second printing appeared in 1989. The most frequently used synopsis of the original Greek text is Kurt Aland, *Synopsis quattuor Evangeliorum*, Stuttgart, 1985 (13th edition), 590 pp.

2　All this information can be found, worked out in greater detail, in the Synopsis by A. Denaux – M. Vervenne mentioned above.

3　Luke begins his gospel as follows, 'Inasmuch as many have undertaken to compile a *narrative* of the things which have been accomplished among us ...' (Lk 1:1). The italicized word 'narrative' is the translation of the Greek word *diêgêsis* meaning description, explanation, story. Luke seems to refer to stories about Jesus composed before his own and which he uses in writing his. Such (fragmentary) stories or *diegese* served, according to this theory, as a source for the three synoptic evangelists.

4　The article published by Karl Lachmann in 1835 was entitled *De ordine narrationum in evangeliis synopticis* [The order of the narratives in the synoptic gospels]. Wilke's work was entitled *Der Urevangelist, oder exegetisch-critische Untersuchung über das Verwandtschaftsverhältnis der drei ersten Evangelien* [*The proto-evangelist, or the critical and exegetical investigation of the interrelationship of the first three gospels*]. Holzmann's most important study was *Die synoptischen Evangelien. Ihr Ursprung und ihr geschichtlicher Charakter* [*The synoptic gospels. Their origin and their historical character*].

5   For example there is the difficult problem known technically as the 'minor agreements'. It concerns the problem of a number of smaller agreements between Matthew and Luke against Mark. These can be negative, i.e. in a few small texts found only in Mark which thus comprise his *Sondergut* (e.g. the parable of the seed in Mk 4:26-29; the healing of the deaf-mute in Mk 7:32-37); or positive, namely, when Matthew and Luke use the same turn of phrase or expression while differing from Mark (see Mt 5:13 and Lk 14:34 'if the salt has lost its taste...', against Mk 9:50 'if the salt has lost its saltiness...'). These minor agreements cause difficulties for the two-source theory, for if Matthew and Luke both use Mark as a basic text, how can we explain that they sometimes agree with one another on minor details while differing from Mark? Proponents of the two-source theory consider most minor agreements coincidental results of editorial changes made by Matthew and Luke to Mark's text. Some think the minor agreements show that Matthew and Luke did not use our present gospel of Mark as it now stands but rather a 'proto-Mark', in other words, an older (lost) version which Mark used as a model.

5

The gospel of Mark

Author, place and date of origin

The second gospel does not name its author. In this the four gospels agree with one another. According to Papias (see above p. 94) *Mark* is the author of the second gospel. The ancient Church and the whole of tradition agree with this judgement. This Mark has always been identified with the John Mark mentioned in the Acts of the Apostles and in some letters, a companion of Paul, and later in Rome of Peter. (For text references see above p. 94). There is no compelling argument for denying this identification. In other words, it is quite possible that tradition is correct here. Yet there are a number of exegetes who prefer, for well-grounded reasons, to speak of an anonymous Christian. The question of the author's identity is also raised when we ask about the origin of the Marcan material. Mark's gospel has often been considered the reflection of Peter's preaching, and in this sense the gospel receives a special stamp as the eye-witness and singular recollections of the 'prince of the apostles'. Now, it cannot be excluded that some of the material did indeed come from Peter's preaching. A number of the gospel's internal characteristics can support this tradition. There is, for example, the graphic narrative style less influenced by literary reworking than is the case with the other gospels. There is also Peter's prominent (and far from flattering) role and the continuous emphasis on the apostles' and disciples' lack of understanding (shown differently than in Matthew). These and similar elements point to a vital and close contact with the preaching and recollections of the apostles themselves. But they do not point compellingly in Peter's direction as such. R. Pesch even writes, 'the supposition that Mark used special Petrine traditions cannot be thought probable...' and R. Brown writes, 'The attitude toward Peter in the second gospel makes it highly unlikely that a disciple of Peter, John Mark, wrote it.'[1]

In any case, for exegetes one thing is certain, even if Peter was a possible source for Mark, he was certainly not the only one. Some exegetes believe they can find some Pauline characteristics (e.g. emphasis on crucifixion theology). P. Van den Berghe summarizes the question as follows:

> Even those who accept Papias' testimony admit that Peter could not have been Mark's only source. The best way to look at the question is to say that Mark's gospel reflects a broad apostolic preaching in which beside voices such as Peter's and Paul's, others less known to us can be heard (ms. course on the synoptics, 1879-9, p. 4).

Taken as a whole, the identification of the author of the second gospel with John Mark remains possible. There are no compelling arguments against the tradition on that point and a number of elements in the gospel text could even point to someone who had lived and worked in the proximity of Peter and Paul. But this question is perhaps less important. As we will see later Matthew is also most likely an anonymous Christian. Furthermore, the traditional identification does not teach us much about the second gospel, since outside what we find in the gospel text we learn nothing about Mark's person except his name. This brings us to a point more important for the question of authorship than knowing a name, i.e. *what does the gospel itself reveal of its author?* Who Mark is, how he thinks, what sources he may have used and how he edited them, all this we must learn by studying the text itself (by 'internal criticism').

There is also no absolute certainty about the *place* where the gospel was written. Since the time of Clement of Alexandria (ca. 200) it has been a firm tradition in the Church that Mark wrote his gospel in Rome. The gospel text does not itself either confirm or disprove this. In any case, there is nothing in the gospel that argues against placing it in Rome. The many words the gospel borrows from Latin (centurion, legion, speculator, praetorian, etc.) could even be an argument in its favour, but it is also true that these Latin words (especially those relating to trade and the military) were used throughout the Roman empire.

Much more important than the exact place is the question of the gospel's intended *audience*. Put differently, to situate the second gospel it is important to have an answer to the question *for what type of people was the gospel written?* To this we can give the following answer:

– Mark's gospel is written for *Christians*, thus for 'intramural use'. It is not a text intended to serve for convincing or proselytizing outsiders. The Christian framework is so evident that someone was able to develop the thesis that Mark's gospel was designed from the beginning for Christian liturgical use, namely to be read as a whole during the Easter service, something in the style of the Jewish 'passover haggada'. This latter is far from certain but that Christians were the recipients of the gospel need not be doubted.

– From the text it appears that the Christians to whom the gospel is addressed live in a *difficult situation*. The faith to which Jesus calls is not a calm, safe, self-evidently socially accepted faith, but a faith that has to struggle to maintain its existence amid opposition, incomprehension and persecution. The emphasis the evangelist puts on incomprehension and opposition with regard to the Messiah plays an important role here.

– The gospel, without doubt, is addressed to *gentile Christians*. The majority of the gospel's audience do not come from Judaism, but have a pagan background. Typical Jewish or Jewish-Christian characteristics such as are found in abundance in Matthew's gospel or in Luke's infancy narrative are almost totally absent in Mark. Even stronger, the evangelist has to explain Jewish customs to his readers (see Mk 7:3f) and Aramaic words are regularly translated (see Mk 3:17; 5:41; 14:36; 15:22...). The addition of a reference to a woman in Jesus' saying on divorce in Mark 10:12 also reflects a gentile-Christian environment.

– The *date* when Mark's gospel was written can be determined with a fairly great certainty. The elements which play a role in dating a gospel have naturally become more numerous and more complex since we have become aware that a gospel tells us as much about its community of origin as it does about Jesus. Regarding Mark's gospel, there is a growing consensus that the text was written during the time of the Roman-Jewish war and the destruction of Jerusalem, thus around the year 70. But this period is what is known as a chronological 'fork' – the interval between two eras – which has so far not been solved satisfactorily. The discussion concerns the interpretation of chapter 13, Jesus' apocalyptic discourse. No one doubts that we have here some references to the situation during the Jewish war, but it is not certain whether Mark knew about the destruction of the temple. Compare, for example, Mk 13 with the version in Lk 21 where it is apparent that Jerusalem has already been destroyed. (See especially Mk 13:14 and Lk 21:20,24. Luke's allusions to the siege and conquest of Jerusalem are much clearer. On this point see also the discussion of Luke's gospel below.) According to some authors Mark wrote during the last phase of the Jewish war *before* the destruction of the temple; in that case the gospel must be dated between 66 and 70. According to others he wrote his gospel in the first years *after* the destruction, thus between 70 and 72/73. Conclusion: we are safe in dating Mark somewhere between 66 and 73 of the common era.

Mark's editorial contribution

Mark's gospel, which still has but a humble place in traditional catechesis, has taken a giant step forward since the breakthrough of the two-source theory. Mark has, in a manner of speaking, been promoted from being the 'little brother' to being the 'father' of Matthew and Luke. One of the leading exegetes of our time, Joachim Gnilka, wrote in the introduction to his great commentary on Mark that:

Mark stands at the end of a process of tradition and at the beginning of the gospel literature and marks as such the transition. Before him lies the process of the oral transmission of the Jesus-tradition in preaching, catechesis, liturgy

125

and diverse forms of early Christian community life covering a period of about forty years; after him Matthew, Luke and John as well as later apocryphal authors will adopt and further develop the gospel genre created by Mark.[2]

These words clearly illustrate Mark's importance. In chapter 3 we saw how traditions about Jesus (stories about and words of Jesus) had been separately and casually circulated in the young communities. We also saw how even in the early decades small *collections* of the words of and the stories about Jesus had come to be, as well as larger units such as the passion narrative and the *Quelle*. But we may believe that it was Mark who was the first to gather the small units of tradition into a *continuous story with a biographical slant*. Using the general (and undoubtedly correct) recollection of the progress of Jesus' public life, namely, his activity in Galilee and his death in Jerusalem – recollections which were present in many of the stories in circulation – Mark created a very simple *frame* for collecting all the stories in one whole. He has Jesus' activities proceed according to this clear outline:

– Preparation for the mission, in Judea (baptism in the Jordan and stay in the desert)
– The mission in Galilee
– The journey to Jerusalem
– Death and discovery of the empty tomb in Jerusalem.

We only have to compare this outline with the outline of John's gospel to notice its simplicity. In John, Jesus is continually travelling back and forth between Jerusalem and Galilee. It is quite possible that John's description more closely approximates the historical reality and that Mark's very simple framework – once in Galilee, once in Jerusalem – is artificial and has a theological and catechetical function. Since Matthew and Luke used Mark, we find in their gospels the same simple (one year?) outline.

Mark included the traditional materials available to him in this framework and created a running story by joining them together with connecting phrases and techniques (e.g. by including references to time). It may be said that he was quite successful and that his gospel, when read straight through, does appear to be a united whole. But whoever looks closely at the text easily notices that many of the scenes had originally existed separately and have been welded together with editorial connections. This explains why we can so easily divide a gospel (at least a synoptic gospel) in separate pericopes each of which forms a small unit when separated from the general context and why these units are quite understandable and easily delimited. The Church has always profited in the liturgy from this ability to make divisions easily as we see from the Sunday readings. Of course Jesus did not tell all the parables of the seed all at once in immediate succession (see Mk 4:1-34); nor did he hold a continuous series of controversies on the relationship of his authority to the Law (see Mk 2:13-27). In such cases we obviously have to do with small collection of pericopes 'ordered by theme' by the evangelist or possible by the tradition before him. In just these two examples the loose and vague connectives between the pericopes show that they had once been told independently of one another. Note in these examples (and also elsewhere in Mark) the many trite commonplace connections such as 'And another time...'; 'Once when...'; 'Once...'; 'On another occasion...'; 'Further...'; etc. See 2;13,15,18,23; 3:1 or 4:1,21,26,30.

Mark's role in fusing and structuring the traditional material is difficult to overestimate. Mark has, as it were, sewn together the many small pieces he received from tradition into one garment (even if many of the seams are clearly visible!). There is still much discussion about his exact position as author toward the traditional material. According to some authors closely related to the earlier school of form criticism, Mark worked very conservatively in structuring the material. This is the opinion of Rudolf Pesch who has reconstructed a preceding 'proto-gospel' from the material in Mark's gospel (*Evangelium der Urgemeinde*, see above p. 80 n. 7). Mark's narrative style which seems more 'primitive' than Matthew's or Luke's (Mark has more of a folk style, is more descriptive, often more clumsy and less regulated than his fellow's), speaks in favour of an unadapted copying of the tradition as such. In this case Mark would only be passing on tradition limiting his own contribution to providing a general structure and connective elements.

But many modern authors with more explicit attention for the sacred writers' personal editorial contributions attribute to Mark a much more creative position than does form criticism. They see in Mark not only the creator of the framework that holds his gospel together, but also the author of some of the narrative material and of the composition (i.e. especially the placing and reworking) of the discourse material. In either case we cannot deny that Mark has given a personal theological view to the gospel and that there are also conscious adaptations made to suit the situation in his Church community. But here too we cannot always be sure how much he adopts from his traditions and how much he creates. Since we are unable to decipher any older stage than Mark for most of the gospel stories, the differences of opinion will not soon disappear. In general, exegetes have no doubt that Mark received the greatest part of the gospel material from tradition. *How* he reworked it, whether conservatively or creatively, that is where the discussion starts.

The structure Mark gave his gospel to make it one continuous story has without doubt played an important theological role and has even determined for the most part the Church's coherent image of Christ. Is not seeing (or creating) coherent relationships one of the most important factors of historical interpretation? Even in daily life the meaning of things and words is only clear in so far as we see how they are connected. A good historian will try to highlight the internal coherence of events in structuring his work and in so doing will try to reveal their meaning. It is obvious that the selection and interpretation of data plays an inescapable role and that purely 'objective' historiography, i.e. historiography that leaves events to their pure, uninterpreted coincidence without creating or mentioning any coherence, is in fact impossible. This would not even be historiography but unordered chaotic literature. On the other side, we must always be aware that what we know and understand of history is what historians have *said* about history. This is also the case for Mark. Our knowledge of Jesus is for a large part filtered by Mark's view of Jesus. Looked at from the point of view of faith, there is no objection to this; it is an essential aspect of the incarnation and of the ecclesiality (i.e. the Church community and dialogical character) of the faith. Were this not the case then God himself and not the prophets would have had to write the prophesies, and Jesus himself would have had to write the gospel, which in any case he did not do. It would not contribute anything essential to the real question of faith.

In Mark the *structural elements* fulfil the function of giving meaning. We provide a few examples:

– The *chronological structure* which consists in joining the facts with references to time (See Mk 1:16,19,21,29,32,35), allow the reader to see rather quickly where Jesus' actions are leading, namely, to his rejection and death in Jerusalem. Mark's chronological indications also contribute to the conspicuously 'hurried' character of his gospel. Mark shows a striking preference for the connecting word *euthus* which can be translated 'right away, soon, immediately, and when, at once...' (See Mk 1:10,12,18,20,21,23,29,30,42,43). When reading Mark we receive somewhat the impression that everything happened very quickly. Mark drags us, as it were, by the hand toward the concluding events in Jerusalem. We have no time to stop and catch our breath.

– The *geographical structure* reveals itself in its simplicity as a remarkable theological instrument. In Mark's gospel there is a sharp contrast between Galilee and Jerusalem. The 'inferior' province of Galilee from which so little can be expected will be the stage for Jesus' expanding activity, while Jerusalem, where the Messiah must be recognized and honoured, appears as the seat of unbelief, refusal and rejection. We have to do here with a clear example of the way in which an evangelist writes history (for Jesus' efficacy in Galilee is plainly historical) as symbol. This contrast is related to the contrast between Jew and gentile. In gentile areas – the other side of the sea of Tiberias, Tyre and Sidon – Jesus meets faith, but among his own Jewish authorities much unbelief. This last characteristic is found in all the gospels. It reflects in part the tragic division between Jew and gentile with regard to Christ's message.

≥ – The leitmotifs which serve as connecting themes in Mark's gospel are also important structural elements. They too draw theological lines, some of which are very important. Among these themes the most striking are perhaps:

– the theme of the disciples' lack of understanding which keeps them from seeing what Jesus is all about (See 4:40; 5:52; 8:17-21; 8:33; 9:10,32. Matthew greatly weakens this theme and occasionally reverses it);

– the theme of the ever increasing number of people coming to Jesus, with Jesus' related and unsuccessful attempts to withdraw from the masses (see 1:28; 1:35-37,45; 2:1f; 3:20; 5:21; 6:31-34,53-66);

– the theme of the journeying Jesus. Jesus is always on the move and is moving in ever expanding circles of activity. First he goes to all the villages of Galilee, then to all the gentile territories surrounding it and then finally to Jerusalem. From this last journey Luke will create an important theological theme for his gospel. (For Mark see 1:14-16,38-39; 3:7; 4:35; 5:1,21; 6:1,6b,45,53; 7:24,31; 8:22-27; 9:30; 10:1,17,32,46; 11:1.);

– the theme of the prediction of Jesus' passion and especially the theme of the so-called hidden Messiah are treated below.

– Just as the structure of a vault is borne by the arches that span it, so is Mark's gospel borne by a number of fields of tension. One such field is *the people's recognition of Jesus' true dignity* (see 1:27f; 2:12; 4:41; 5:20; 7:37 etc.). Another closely related to the first is the *progressive heavenly revelation of Jesus' dignity* at his baptism (1:11), transfiguration (9:7) and death and resurrection (15:33,38; 16:6-7). The most important and comprehensive field – we could also speak of 'line of meaning' – is the *way of the Son of man*, which Mark most likely borrowed from tradition. He modelled his whole gospel on it. The whole gospel seems to be the 'way of the Son of man', a way which starts with the mission of John the Baptist announced by the prophets and passes through Galilee to Jerusalem, but returns from there to Galilee where Jesus goes before his disciples as the risen Lord. This latter leads to the formation of the Christian community so that the way of the Son of man

130

ends in fact in Mark's Church... or, for us, who now read the gospel, in our Churches. ≤

Some of Mark's main themes

The whole of Mark's gospel is focused on the *passion*. The German exegete Martin Kähler once called Mark's gospel 'a passion narrative with a long introduction'. Although this is somewhat exaggerated, it is still an adequate approach to the second gospel, for it is true that Jesus' passion casts its shadow over the whole gospel. We refer here to texts such as Mk 3:6; 8:31ff and 10:32ff. Beside the predictions of Jesus' passion there are other themes closely connected to the passion narrative such as the suffering of John the Baptist who was in this too Jesus' 'precursor' (see Mk 1:14; 6:14-29; 9:11-13 where with Elijah John the Baptist is meant); and Jesus' summons to his disciples to follow him in his suffering (8:34-9:1; 9:35-37; 10:38-40,42-45; compare 15:21 with Jn 19:17 where Jesus carries his own cross). It will not have been by accident that it was said of Bartimaeus, 'Jesus said to him, "Go your way, your faith has made you well." And immediately he received his sight and followed him on the way' (10:52). He whose eyes have been opened by faith, followed Jesus on his journey to... the passion. It can seem strange (and superfluous?) to us Christians in this day and age who grew up with the fixed image of Jesus' life which the gospels offer us that we speak here of a theological theme in Mark. For us it seems evident that Jesus' life, as it were, from its very beginning was directed toward and grew toward the passion. But we may not forget that this was not so for Jesus' contemporaries. It was not immediately clear either for Jesus' disciples or for his opponents where his life was leading as it is not clear for any human life. In this sense Jesus' life was no more 'planned' than ours is. It is mainly due to Mark's structuring work that we now look at his life from the single perspective of the passion. It is a viewpoint created 'after the fact'.

In this way Mark's gospel offers a *crucifixion theology*. It is for this reason that there is even discussion of Pauline influence in Mark. For us this latter is not necessary, but in any case Mark's gospel continually points out to the reader the *scandal* of the Christians' conviction, i.e. that they believed in a Messiah who was crucified and eliminated rather than one who has come to put affairs immediately in order in this world. The gospel is written completely from the confession that the crucified Jesus is the Messiah – for he was risen – but it wants to continually warn Christians against a too cheap and triumphalist faith in Christ. The Messiah *has been crucified*, and whoever wants to follow him must be aware of this.

In an excellent article on Mark's crucifixion theology,[3] Frans Lefevre writes:

> Mark not only wants to preach that Jesus is the Messiah, but more strongly – and this puts an undeniably different accent – that *this crucified* Jesus is the Messiah. Mark says, 'Do not think too quickly, readers, that you know who Jesus is and what it means to be his follower.' His readers – and we may add, Jesus' own disciples – used the generally current understanding of the concept 'Messiah' or 'Son of God' and applied it to Jesus. But Mark says, 'No, do not think that what Jesus is becomes so very obvious from these titles. It is just the opposite. The meaning of 'Messiah' or 'Son of God' only becomes clear from a correct understanding of Jesus. Speak therefore *none too quickly* about Jesus in the classical style. That is only possible when all misunderstandings are excluded, only when you see all that Jesus said and did (namely, all those famous miracles told of him) *in the light of the cross*. Or as Jesus said when coming down from the mountain, only 'when the Son of man has *risen from the dead...*'.

Mark warns against all triumphalism.

> Only under the cross where the one dimensionality of triumphant cheering is totally excluded do we hear unambiguously the paradoxical confession of the gentile Church that the Son

of God is no one less than the one condemned, that *this crucified* person is (still) the Messiah.

Here we have already touched on another of Mark's themes that is an aspect of this crucifixion theology, the theme of the *hidden Messiah* or the *hidden Son of God*. The second term is better than the first, because the secret is more related to the title 'Son of God', but the first term is generally accepted usage and is not incorrect. The hidden Son of God is an intriguing theme in Mark's gospel.

≥ In general we see Jesus forbidding others to tell about his miracles (he is not successful) see 1:44; 5:43; 7:36. A closer look shows that his prohibition must have something to do with revealing his identity. He forbids the evil spirits to speak 'because they knew him' (cf 1:24f; 1:34; 3:11f). The same happens with his disciples at important moments of revelation, see 8:29-30; 9:7-9. And finally we learn that Jesus' identity is expressed in the term, 'Son of God' (or the 'Son of the Most High'; for Mark the term Christ is practically synonymous with this. This last is quite normal given its Jewish background, since even in the Old Testament the 'Anointed' or 'Messiah' – *Christos* in Greek – the king of Israel was called the 'Son of God'. See Ps 2:7). See Mk 1:11; 3:11f; 5:7; 9:7-9. That Mark's gospel revolves around the *identity of the Son of God* is clear from the whole text. The divine revelations at his baptism and transfiguration (Word of God stories) call Jesus the Son, the Sanhedrin condemns him on the basis of this title (14:61-64), and when all has been completed – when the curtain in the temple, the centre of Jewish messianic expectations, is rent because the Holy of Holies is now to be found on Golgotha – the centurion says 'Truly, this man was the Son of God!' *After* the crucifixion. The title of Mark's gospel is, 'The beginning of the gospel of Jesus [the] Christ, *the Son of God'*. ≤

Why all the secrecy? In the prohibition against speaking of his miracles and in the prohibition against revealing his identity the same theme is active which we have already met in the crucifixion theology, namely, that before Jesus had followed his mission to the end and been rejected and crucified – also meaning been excommunicated from the community of Israel as People of God – the confession 'You are the Son of God' can only cause misunderstanding. The disciples lack of understanding when faced with predictions of Jesus' suffering illustrate this abundantly. The healings will only cause people to run after Jesus as a miracle worker, as someone who 'proves' he is the Son of God because of his spectacular deeds and *not* Son of God in the sense in which he really wants to be understood (cf Jn 6:14-15,26). Using D. Bonhoeffer's terms we could not say they would run after him as an image of God who functions as a stop-gap for human weakness.

This means that the miracles which Mark nevertheless relates in abundance do *not* have the apologetic function of 'proving Jesus' divinity', but must be read as signs that God's saving, liberating and forgiving nearness is present among people in Jesus. For this reason Jesus, the great miracle worker, can say with a sigh, 'Why does this generation seek a sign? Truly, I say to you, no sign shall be given to this generation' (Mk 8:12).

A premature revelation of his identity by the demons (i.e. before his crucifixion) would only cause an incorrect view of his identity. That Jesus' identity as Son of God could not agree with the fixed opinion which then prevailed about what the Messiah should be, is illustrated with the most tragic irony by the fact that the high priest and the Sanhedrin (who *should* have seen, as John will later continually emphasize) reject and crucify him, while the centurion (a gentile who is not expected to have seen) utters a confession of faith under the very cross, 'Truly, this was the Son of God.' This utterance is at the same time an immediate confirmation of the gentiles in Mark's community.

As F. Lefevre says, Mark is always flashing 'warning lights' to avoid an erroneous view of Jesus' Sonship. The much-loved Son who saw the heavens rent and the Spirit descend upon him, had to go immediately into the desert to be tested by Satan (1:12-13). The disciples, totally dumbfounded by the transfiguration, are told by the voice from heaven calling them to follow, 'listen to him' (9:7) with immediately thereafter an allusion to the suffering already undergone by John the Baptist which the disciples – as usual – do not understand (9:9-13). Add to this the summons to follow the cross, the disciples manifest inability to understand their master's true intentions, Peter's boasting and betrayal during the passion..., and the function of the hidden Messiah theme is clear, i.e. *before* experiencing the cross – the failure – Mark's readers cannot in truth confess that Jesus is the Son of God, or even know *which* Son of God they want to follow, for they remain entangled in triumphalistic misunderstanding.

What was true of Jesus' disciples is also true for Mark's community and for anyone from any era who wants to follow Christ. People can only learn to know Christ, not when taking or receiving power as even the apostles had hoped (Mk 10:35-45!), but when they will take up the cross to carry it behind him as Simon of Cyrene.

All this shows that the central theme in Mark is *christology*. The whole gospel revolves around the question *who is this man?* It is a question asked by the people, the authorities and the disciples, by the Jews and by the gentiles. The purpose of the whole gospel is to give christological content to the titles in the first verse. In other words, the evangelist begins his writing by stating that Jesus is the Christ and the Son of God, but *the story that follows will show what is to be understood by this*. Mark does not present the content of these titles in the style of a dogmatic tract with definitions and arguments, but in the style of a story or even more of a drama.

How Jesus is the Son of God and the Anointed, that is what we learn to suspect and ultimately to see and confess throughout the drama that puts him among people: his disciples, his family, the masses, the opponents in Jerusalem. The purpose of the second gospel's whole structure is to serve this 'christological drama' which will be developed much more strongly and intensely in John.

It was necessary to spend some extra time on Mark's editorial structure and its theological importance because it is so important for an understanding of the *three synoptics*. Since Matthew and Luke took Mark's gospel as the basis for their writings, we find in them too the same structural elements and same theological patterns. We will not discuss these further in the following pages. Rather, we will highlight only the characteristics which separate Matthew and Luke from Mark and which determine their uniqueness.

NOTES

1 R. Pesch, *Das Marcusevangelium* [*The gospel of Mark*] in the series HTKNT, 3rd edition, Freiburg, 1980, vol. 1, p. 10. Pesch writes further, 'the way in which Mark *edited* the traditions available to him [– and it is just in the editing that the evangelist's individual identity is highlighted –] does not particularly prove him to be from Palestine or Jerusalem nor a disciple of Peter.' He concludes, 'We must resign ourselves to accepting that we know from tradition only that the author of the second gospel had the not infrequent name Mark' (*op. cit.*, p. 11). R. Brown, *The Community of the Beloved Disciple*, N.Y./Ramsey/Toronto: Paulist Press, 1979, p. 34 n. 46.

2 J. Gnilka, *Das Evangelium nach Marcus* [*The gospel according to Mark*] in Ekknt, Zurich: Neukirchen-Vluyn, 1978, vol. 1., p. 17.

3 F. Lefevre, 'Het Marcusevangelium als mysterie van het Kruis' [*The Gospel of Mark as Mystery of the Cross*] in *Collationes* 11 (1981), pp. 10f.

6

The gospel of Matthew

Author, place and date of origin

The first gospel was traditionally considered the oldest of the gospels. It has from antiquity borne the name Matthew with which was unanimously meant the apostle Matthew, the tax collector, one of the twelve. According to Papias' testimony, the apostle Matthew ordered the Lord's words (*logia*)[1] in Hebrew (= Aramaic). The present gospel of Matthew is to have been a Greek translation of this Aramaic gospel of Matthew (see above p. 94). But what did Papias mean with these *logia*?

Modern literary criticism has unanimously agreed that Matthew's gospel in its present form is *not* a translation from a Hebrew or Aramaic writing, but that it was written directly in Greek. If Papias' expression '*logia* of the Lord' refers to a real document, then it is not an Aramaic original version of our present gospel. If the basic choices made by the two-source theory are correct, then we know that Matthew's main source was Mark's gospel. The document to which Papias refers would have to involve other, non-Marcan material. Many Bible scholars think it advisable to accept the idea that behind the present gospel of Matthew there lies a semitic (Hebrew or Aramaic) document containing mainly (or even exclusively?) *logia* in the strict sense, i.e. 'words of Jesus' and that Papias meant *that* document when he speaks of *ta logia*. If Papias' testimony is to be trusted and does refer to a written document then this document might possibly be identified with an Aramaic *Quelle* text. We know that the *Quelle* must have been of Palestinian origin.

It is not necessary to explain the two-source theory again here. When we accept on philological grounds that the present gospel of Matthew was written directly in Greek; when we can also discover that it is not the work of a first-hand eye-witness but of *someone who is dependent on sources*, in particular on Mark as main source (who has thus determined the structure of Matthew's gospel) with Q as secondary source, then we are compelled to conclude that the *author* of the first gospel cannot be identified with the Galilean apostle Matthew (or Levi). We will probably never know who he was.

As is the case with the other gospels, we are unable to name with certainty the *place* where Matthew's gospel was written. From the gospel itself we are led to think mostly of Syria or Palestine, favouring Syria somewhat over Palestine; perhaps the Syrian capital, Antioch, perhaps some Christian community located more to the south. The place of origin was mostly likely a Christian community still close to the Jewish sphere of influence. For Matthew's gospel too an important question in this regard is, *for whom was this document written*? From internal criticism we can, in general lines, give the following answer:

– The gospel must have been written by a *Jewish-Christian author* for a community consisting primarily in *Christians of Jewish origin*. A number of the gospel's characteristics point in this direction such as (i) the great emphasis on fulfilling the Scriptures and the concern to portray Jesus as someone whose behaviour did not contravene the *Torah* (the Law) but rather as someone who has come to fulfil the Law and the Prophets and who may be seen as the new Moses; (ii) the evangelist's familiarity with the rabbinical method of interpreting Scripture and treating typical rabbinical questions (see Mt 5:31f; 6:1-6,16-18); (iii) the fact that Jewish customs were not explained (Compare Mt 15:2 with Mk 7:27; Mt 26:17 with Mk 14:12); (iv) the fact that several Hebrew words are used without translation (e.g. 5:22 *raca;* 10:25 *Beelzebub;* 27:6 *Corban.* Compare Mk 7:11).

Matthew's Christian community is *in conflict with official Judaism*. This is a suitable moment for a sketch of the situation in that period.

In 66 the Jews revolted against their Roman over-lords. After a bloody war, the later Roman emperor Titus conquered Jerusalem in the year 70 and destroyed the temple. Thousands of Jews were killed or sold into slavery. Judaism's very chance to survive was at risk. A few Pharisees (after the year 70, we hear no more about Sadducees), shortly before the drama in Jerusalem, withdrew to Jamnia (now called Javna), a place just south of modern Tel-Aviv. There they formed a new type of Sanhedrin or permanent synod. From there they will try to save and reorganize the Jewish culture and religion. Since the preservation of their faith and their religious identity are threatened, the Pharisees will follow a policy of clear, strict demarcations. Internally they strove for a greater unity in the Jewish faith which led to the fixing of the Old Testament canon. Externally they erected barriers against all movements and groups which could endanger the identity of the Jewish religion. Among such groups the Pharisees of Jamnia included the 'innovative' Christians who, in venerating Jesus as Messiah, in their indolence in following the Law of Moses, in their openness to gentiles, etc, did much harm to Jewish affairs.

This increasing strictness will negatively influence the already difficult relations between Christians and official Judaism. In the period after 70 a deep break occurred between Christians and Judaism. The Christians, many of whom continued to attend the synagogue, were now excluded. In the Jewish Eighteen Benedictions, a part of synagogue worship, an invocation was added against *minim*, i.e. heretics (also referred to as slanderers and malefactors) which referred among others also to Christians.[2] From then on Judaism considered Christianity a rejected sect. Read here Mt 10:17 and 23:34 and note the words 'their' and 'your' synagogues. Jesus' disciples no longer belong there! Etienne Charpentier is very probably correct when he says that Jesus' unusually hard attacks against the Pharisees (Mt 23) come perhaps less from the earthly Jesus of the year 30 than from Risen Christ, living in the community of the 80's and that the attacks are directed toward Phariseeism in Jamnia.[3] This could be a good example of the adaptation of the Jesus tradition to the local community situation (a small part of the discourse against the Pharisees comes from the triple tradition, a large part from Q, but some is also from SgMt). In Matthew's gospel we do indeed continually hear echoes of the Christian faith's self-defense against Jewish accusations. See, for example, some remarkable 'apologetic' passages on this matter (Mt 27:62-66 and 28:11-15 – SgMt) in the appearance stories.

– There is no doubt that Matthew's community has accepted gentiles in its midst and is *open to the mission to the gentiles*. Matthew's community reads in the mission to the gentiles Jesus' desire for mission. Whereas Jesus' mission was on the whole limited to Israel (Mt 10:5-6) the success of the mission to the gentiles is seen as the fulfilment of a task assigned by the Risen Lord, 'Go therefore and make disciples of all nations' (Mt 28:18-20).

As to the *time* when Matthew's gospel was written, it has to have been at a moment when Mark's gospel was already sufficiently distributed and in a period of polemic between Christianity and Judaism. The acrimony of the polemic indicates that the separation must still have been 'fresh' – one does not defend one's self so sharply against an opponent with whom there has been no contact in a long time. For this reason most modern exegetes think it was written between the years 80 and 90.

Matthew's editorial contribution

Much more than in Mark, we meet in Matthew an effort to *systematize* the material (Mk + Q + SgMt). His gospel demonstrates more closely than Mark's the character of a closed composition. One of the evangelist's peculiarities is that from chapters 3 up to and including 13 he is rather free in re-arranging Mark's ordering of the pericopes, but that from chapter 14 onward he follows it rather slavishly. This has to do with his editorial work.

We see that Matthew has the tendency to bring together in more or less closed units material related in form and content. Very striking is the clear demarcation of *five discourses of Jesus* which, as it were, support the gospel as five pillars. We find in Matthew's gospel, at regular intervals from one another, five discourses which the evangelist consciously designed as such. Each of the five is introduced by stereotypical formulas such as,

'And when Jesus finished these sayings (words, lessons)...',
before he allows his story to continue. See Mt 7:28; 11:1; 13:53;
19:1; 26:1.

And so we have:

1.	The sermon on the mount	5:1(3)-7:29
2.	The mission discourse	10:1(15)-11:1
3.	The parable discourse	13:1(4)-11:1
4.	The ecclesiastical discourse	18:1(3)-19:1
5	The apocalyptic discourse	24:1(4)-26:1

The narrative units are to be found in between these discourses. According to some authors it is possible that Matthew
planned *a discourse + a narrative section as a unit*. We can
illustrate this using chapters 5-9. We have the impression that
the whole of this section (sermon on the mount + miracles) is
intentionally put in a framework between two nearly identical
sentences which reflect Jesus' general activity. In 4:23, just
before 5:1, we read the following summarizing overview (we
call such an overview a *summarium*) of Jesus' activities, 'And
he went about all Galilee, teaching in their synagogues and
preaching the gospel of the kingdom and healing every disease
and every infirmity among the people'. In 9:25 after the sermon
on the mount and a first section with miracles we read a nearly
identical sentence as conclusion. Be aware that the evangelists
were not responsible for the division into chapters nor the num-
bering of the verses, so that both these sentences really 'encap-
sulate' the text in chapters 5-9. In exegesis we call such a device
inclusio (inclusion – as between parentheses). We get the impression that Matthew intended here to present these five chapters as a single unit, and in so doing to show that the kingdom of
God which Jesus proclaims in the sermon on the mount (5-7) is
achieved in his healing and liberating activity (8-9). There are
exegetes who see the whole architecture of Matthew's gospel
analogously constructed on the basis of five 'blocks' edited in
pairs (i.e. a discourse + a narrative section).[4] Whether or not
Matthew himself consciously composed such a tight structure

cannot be proven and is disputed. But the clear delineation of the five discourses which does seem to divide the gospel into five main parts remains a remarkable compositional element of the first gospel.

The grouping of Jesus' words in five long discourses brings us to another important Matthean trait. In Matthew more than in the other gospels, Jesus appears as a real rabbi, *as a teacher*.

Since these discourses are clearly a Matthean editorial device, many exegetes are convinced that the evangelist himself must have been a teacher. Many believe that the well known – and unusual – saying in Mt 13:52 could be a small self-portrait (an autobiographical note). Matthew could himself be the scribe trained for the kingdom of heaven 'who brings out of his treasure what is new and what is old', i.e. that he uses both the Old Testament (which he does do repeatedly) and the new teaching to instruct his Christians. Be it as it may, Matthew is without any doubt the most 'doctrinal' of the four evangelists. Think of the sermon on the mount which formulates a sort of 'constitution' of the kingdom of heaven. The Matthean version of the beatitudes (Mt 5:3-12) offers a perfect example of the fusion of 'old and new'.

≥ The express preference for Jesus' 'teacher' aspect leads Matthew to simplify and shorten the miracle stories in favour of his dogmatic sayings. This makes Matthew's gospel much less 'picturesque' than Mark's. Compare for example, Mt 9:1-8 with Mk 2:1-12 where Mark's lively description of the way the paralytic is brought to Jesus becomes in Matthew just something along the way. Or Mt 8:28-34 with Mk 5:1-17 where Matthew's description of the possessed is much more sober than Mark's rather spectacular version. Compare also Mt 9:18-26 with Mk 5:21-43 and Mt 14:1-12 with Mk 6:14-29. *The simplification of the narratives* (by eliminating what the author apparently considered superfluous detail) is a general tendency in Matthew's gospel. ≤

Main theological characteristics of Matthew's gospel

As we said earlier, we will no longer return to the theological characteristics which Matthew has in common with his source Mark. In so far as he followed Mark in his general structure, Matthew also gives the passion narrative a central place in his gospel, e.g. in Matthew too the predictions of the passion trace out the path of the Son of man. In this section we will limit ourselves to two main concerns of Matthean theology.

Christology

What may perhaps be the two most important characteristics of Matthean christology can be found summarized in the conclusion of his gospel, more specifically in Mt 28:18, 'And Jesus came and said to them *"All authority in heaven and on earth has been given to me"*.' And also in 28:20b *'And lo, I am with you always, to the close of the age.'* It is true that the end of a gospel can teach us much about the author's intentions. This is in any case also true of Luke and John.

All authority in heaven and on earth has been given to me

With this somewhat altered quotation from Dan 7:14 (the vision of the Son of man) Matthew indicates that Jesus is indeed the *Son of man*, the expected and announced *Messiah* and *Son of David*. Matthew's whole gospel intends to show that Jesus is the fulfilment of the hope in the Messiah so dear to the Jews – the hope that incomprehensibly was rejected by his own people, more particularly by their leaders. Matthew's christology is first of all directed toward *Jewish heritage itself*. Jesus is the fulfilment of everything the Scriptures lead us to expect from God. In other words, the gospel's christology is fundamentally directed toward Judaism.

It is for this reason that Matthew puts so much emphasis on

143

the *fulfilment of the Scriptures*. Explicitly or implicitly – we could almost say when it fits and when it does not – the Scriptures are called upon to guarantee what Jesus says and does, or what happens to him. The evangelist not only adopts the old traditional theme of the crucifixion and resurrection 'in accordance with the Scriptures' (1 Cor 15:3f!), but expands this theme to all aspects of Jesus' activity and experience. Read on this Mt 4:15-16; 18:17; 9:13a; 12:17-21 and many other verses. The examples mentioned are particularly interesting because all four show Matthean additions to the triple tradition and thus indicate a personal characteristic of the evangelist.

In this regard we may also refer to Matthew's *infancy narrative*. Matthew and Luke have each separately added an atrium to the material from Mark and *Quelle*. Although thoroughly different from one another and in some places even contradictory – as we said the infancy narratives do not belong to the double tradition but to the *Sondergut* – these two stories have more or less the same purpose. They both want to be 'theological overtures' to the gospel and to show that Jesus was the Messiah from birth. For this both Matthew and Luke use the style of the rabbinical stories about Scripture, the so-called *midrash* stories. Matthew very emphatically wants to show that all that takes place around Jesus' birth is 'in accordance with the Scriptures'. See Mt 1:22-23; 2:5-6; 1:15;17-18,23. See also above p. 32.

≥ That Jesus brings the fulfilment of the Scriptures also influences the way in which Matthew's gospel portrays him in his *relationship to the Law*. Jesus performs as a teacher of the Law. He teaches as a rabbi (but – and Matthew has this from Mark – with another authority than that of the rabbis) and confirms expressly the infrangible faithfulness to the *Torah*. In the sermon on the mount we hear Jesus speak the very conservative sounding words,

Think not that I have come to abolish the law and the prophets; I have come not to abolish them but to fulfil them. For truly, I say to you, till heaven and earth pass away, not an iota, not a dot, will pass from the law until all is accomplished. Whoever then relaxes one of the least of these commandments and teaches men so, shall be called least in the kingdom of heaven; but he who does them and teaches them shall be called great in the kingdom of heaven.

These words are SgMt. But since Jesus has received all authority from God, his interpretation of the *Torah* is normative, even if it contradicts the 'righteousness of the Pharisees'. (Read in this regard Mt 5:20-6:18.) It is not what Jesus says and does that contradicts God's Word – even though it is certain he was historically accused of this – but the activity of those who will reject and kill him in the name of *their* interpretation of the law (read 23:13ff). Jesus is the Messiah and therefore teaches the law according to God's original intention. For this reason Matthew also portrays him as the new and *definitive Moses*. This becomes particularly clear in the sermon on the mount. As Moses proclaimed the Law of the Old Covenant on Mount Sinai, so Jesus teaches on the mount the Law of the kingdom of heaven. The *Torah* of Moses is not repudiated but fulfilled according to its original intentions. The parallelism between the two is even illustrated in the structure of the texts themselves. In Ex 20-23 we read first the basis of the *Torah*, namely, the *Decalogue* or Ten Commandments and then a more extensive 'Book of the Covenant' with many types of concrete regulations. The sermon on the mount, Mt 5-7, calls to mind the same structure. First there is the basis of Jesus' teaching, namely, the Eight Beatitudes and then a more extensive 'Book of the New Covenant', in which a number of concrete cases are mentioned. Many exegetes point out that the parallelism between Moses and Jesus begins even in Matthew's infancy narrative; the murder of the innocent (children), the persecution of Jesus and the flight to Egypt do indeed make us think of Moses and Israel in the beginning of the book of Exodus.

Jesus, just as the Pharisee scribes, also preaches *righteousness*, but the righteousness that Jesus preaches comes forth from pure *grace* and is therefore introduced by the beatitudes (Blessed are the poor of spirit!). This righteousness, which is the righteousness that God desired from the beginning, must be expressed in forms which go much deeper than the Pharisees' legalism and casuistry. (Read the sermon on the mount but especially Mt 5:20-48; also Mt 18 and 23.) The righteousness that Jesus teaches is *universal* (8:5-13; 21:28-22:14). The 'newness' of Jesus' words and attitude consists, according to Matthew, not in that he abrogates the *Torah* and puts other things in its place, but that he *radicalizes* the *Torah*, i.e. brings it back to its roots. That is what reveals him as the one sent by God, and the Messiah. ≤

The fact that Jesus' messianism becomes evident in *the way in which he teaches the Law*, explains why in Matthew's gospel more than in the others the emphasis is put on Jesus' teaching as the guideline for human behaviour (the practice), thus as *ethic*. We find one of the most beautiful illustrations of this in Matthew's beatitudes. When we compare Matthew's beatitudes with those in Luke (Mt 5:3-12 // Lk 6:20-26) we are struck by the enhanced 'moralizing' character of the Matthean version. Since it is Jesus' concern to point the way in righteousness to the kingdom of heaven, Matthew's gospel appears as one large and broad instruction on the new righteousness, as a book of *Christian living*. For Matthew we can correctly speak of an *evangelical ethic*. In comparing Matthew with Mark (where we almost look in vain for moral directives – they come primarily from Q and Sg) this is very striking.

It is above all to this characteristic that the first gospel owes its paramount influence in Church history. Matthew has always been the pre-eminent 'Church gospel' because, in a certain sense, it was the most usable.

Lo, I am with you always, to the close of the age

What was announced at the beginning of the gospel, namely, 'and his name shall be called Emmanuel (which means *God with us*)' (1:23), has been definitively accomplished by virtue of his death and resurrection. At the end of Matthew's gospel Jesus expresses the idea with which the gospel began, 'Lo, I am with you…'. For Matthew this *inclusio* (1:23 and 18:20) is theologically important because it illustrates his view of the resurrection. The whole of Matthew's gospel is written against the belief that Jesus of Galilee and Jerusalem is at the same time also *the Lord who lives in the community*. In living in faith his message, the community experiences the power of the Risen Lord. More so than in the other gospels we receive in reading Matthew the impression that Jesus from Galilee or Jerusalem is actually speaking to Matthew's Christian community or its opponents (see above p. 139, the description of the Pharisees of Jamnia). Put differently, Matthew projects into Jesus' historical life (his group of disciples, his conflicts…) the life of what it is like to be a disciple of Jesus (or opponent of Jesus) in Matthew's own time.

≥ Matthew's Jesus is at a greater distance than the lively recollections still found in Mark. In Matthew Jesus is represented more as 'Lord'. He is more formal, has a hierarchical style. He has been (as in Luke and even more in John) 'literarily reworked'. This is something we notice most often in small details. For example, Matthew has the tendency to eliminate from his description of Jesus any expressions of strong emotion or weakness (compare Mt 8:2-3 with Mk 1:41,43) and to emphasize his power (see 4:23 / 9:35; 15:30). In Mark 6 we see Jesus in his home town Nazareth, where no one believes him. Of this Mark says, 'And he could do no mighty work there, except that he laid his hands upon a few sick and healed them. And he marvelled because of their unbelief.' Whereas Matthew (13:58) turns it into, 'And he did not do many mighty works there, because of their unbelief.' We find the same type of adaptation of Jesus' words in his meeting with the rich young man. In Mk 10:17-18 we read, 'And as he was setting out on his journey, a man ran up and knelt before him, and asked him "Good Teacher, what must I do to inherit eternal life?" and Jesus said to him "Why do you call me good? No one is good but God alone…".' In Matthew Jesus' answer is, 'Why do you ask me about what is good? One there is who is good…' (Mt 19:17). Apparently the words Jesus uses in Mark, 'Why do you call me good?' sound somewhat too humble for Matthew's exalted image of Jesus. Compare also Mt 8:2-3 with Mk 1:41,43 and see Mt 4:23, 9:35, 15:30f. The disciples *worshipped him…* as happens in the Christian communities (28:9,17; cp 2:11). Jesus is the *saviour* of the Christian community in difficulty (cf the combination of the theme of the disciples' following and the story of the storm at sea in Mt 8:18-27, the *master and teacher* of the community (sermon on the mount; ecclesiastical discourse) as well as its *model* (3:15; temptation narrative 4:1-11; 11:28-30 SgMt). ≤

Matthew's view of the Church of ecclesiology

We share the opinion of various exegetes who have pointed out that Matthew is particularly attentive to the continuity between, on the one side, Jesus' proclaiming the kingdom of heaven and, on the other, its accomplishment in the Christian community, i.e. in the Church. This continuity seems to be a sort of theological 'artery' in Matthew's gospel. Charpentier's division as described in note reflects this idea. Such a structure is of course not compulsory and many other divisions of the gospel have also been suggested, but in our opinion it is undeniable that the first gospel continually gives the impression of being not only the story of Jesus but that it is also for the whole time the *story of the Church*. All that happens to the disciples in the gospel, all for which they are being prepared, all that is predicted to them, all this refers to the Christian community listening to the gospel and trying to live it. We can find several indications in the text pointing in this direction, indications which may be called typically Matthean:

– In the gospel the disciples are portrayed in counterpoint with Israel. The Church is the *new Israel* born from the refusal of the old. Jean Zumstein writes, 'The disciples are those who, despite some faults, accept Christ's teaching; they form what Matthew explicitly calls the Church.' This is very typically Matthean. The term church, *ekklesia,* can be found in Mt 16:18 and 18:18. Matthew is the *only* evangelist who uses this term. 16:18 shows very clearly his intention. Peter, who is the first to confess, 'You are the Christ, the Son of the living God', immediately becomes the rock on which the Church will be built. In contrast Israel incarnates opposition, the rejection of Jesus. This rejection culminates in Jesus' death; this makes of Israel an anti-model for the Church.[5]

≥ As to what the Church's most important characteristics and tasks are, Matthew provides some glimpses in his presentation of *Jesus' disciples*.

First of all a disciple is someone who *listens* to what the Lord teaches. The disciples are the first audience of Jesus' five great discourses (see 5:1; 11:1; 13:10,36; 18:1; 24;1,3). They come to Jesus to learn from him. In Matthew there are also many more instructions for the disciples alone than there are in the other gospels. See 9:37-11:1; 13:10-23; 16:24-28, etc.

Directly related to this, the disciple is someone who must *understand* Jesus' teaching. The disciple is above all the one who understands. See 13:51; compare 16:11-12 with Mk 8:20-21 where we see that while Mark preserves Jesus' accusation of the disciples' lack of understanding, Matthew adds to it, 'Then they understood...'. We find the same in Mt 17:13. The evangelist adds to Mark's text, 'Then the disciples understood that he was speaking to them of John the Baptist' (cp Mk 9:11-13). Note also the contrast between the disciples and the people in 13:10-17.

Who has listened and understood will *act according to God's will*. Matthew's gospel is one and all invitation to do God's will. This is particularly evident in the conclusion to the sermon on the mount where Matthew puts the *Quelle* material, 7:13-23,24-27. Jesus' true disciple does not stop only with words but continues on to practice evangelical righteousness in action. Judgement will be based on concrete cases. A very strong example is Mt 25:31-46, the righteous one practices true righteousness (which is love of neighbour); this is sufficient for their inclusion in God's glory even when they are not consciously aware of doing it 'for God', since whatever is done to the least of the brothers is done to Christ! Matthew shows here that he is fully heir to Jewish religious tradition, which unanimously says that the *Torah* is something one must *do*. In this sense he is closely related to the other real 'Jew' among the New Testament authors, namely, the author of the letter of James. See Jas 1:22-25 and 2:14-26. That Matthew has primarily the disciples in mind is evident when reading 12:46-50. Whereas Mark in his narrative (3:33) speaks of 'a crowd [that] was sitting about him', Matthew refers specifically to the disciples; it is they who do the Father's will. *Unconditionally following the Teacher* (see 8:18-27; 4:22) does not consist in calling, 'Lord, Lord' but in *obeying* the Law of the kingdom of heaven, which is none other than that of love, mercy and justice. ≤

NOTES

1   Strictly speaking *'logia'* as used here can also mean 'stories about' Jesus, i.e. stories about what he did. Papias also uses the word to refer to the content of Mark's gospel, and there he clearly refers to what the Lord 'said and *did*'. In our context we need not treat the point in depth concerning Matthew.

2   Still we have to be very careful in interpreting the notorious 'twelfth benediction' from the Eighteen Benedictions. It reads as follows, 'And for slanderers let there be no hope, and let all wickedness perish and let them all be quickly removed. Tear out the arrogant, break them, cast them down, quickly, in our days. Blessed is the Lord who breaks enemies and casts down the arrogant.' See H. Gersh, *The Sacred Books of the Jews*, NY: Stein and Day, 1968, p. 223. The anti-Christian tendency of this prayer has doubtless been exaggerated and often distorted by later Christians. On this see D.J. Van Der Sluis – P.J. Tomson, e.a., 'Elke morgen nieuw. Het Achtiengebed' [New every day, the Eighteen Benedictions] in *Handboek voor de studie van de rabbijnse literatuur* [*Handbook for the study of rabbinical literature*], vol. 1, Folkertsma-Stichting voor Talmudica, 1978, pp. 257-266.

3   E. Charpentier, *Pour lire le Nouveau Testament* [*To Read the New Testament*], p. 69. Many authorities share the same opinion, e.g. James Charlesworth, *Jesus within Judaism*, London, 1989, p. 46, 'The harsh portraits of the Pharisees reflect not so much Jesus' time as the clashes between the Christians and the Pharisees after 70 CE'.

4   Among them Ph. Rolland, J. Radermakers and also E. Charpentier who further divides the structure of Matthew's gospel into two parts in which the parallelism of the kingdom of heaven and the Church is the sustaining force. His divisions are:
Prologue: The mystery of Jesus-Emmanuel (1-2);
Part I: Jesus preaches the kingdom of heaven to all; prepares for the Church (3-16).
Transition from the Old to the New Testament (3-4):
(1) (= first block) the kingdom of heaven has come (sermon on the mount, 5-7; ten miracles, 8-9);
(2) Jesus sends his disciples to preach while continuing himself to do so (mission discourse, 10; Jesus on mission, 11-12);
(3) the decisive choice toward the preaching of the kingdom (parable discourse, 13:1-52; on the way to Peter's confession, 13:53-16:12).

Part II: Jesus makes his Church ready for its task in the kingdom of heaven (17-28)
(4) the kingdom of heaven passes from the Jewish people to the Church (ecclesiastical discourse, 18; from Galilee to Jerusalem, 19-23);
(5) definitive beginning of the kingdom of heaven in the Easter events (apocalyptic discourse, 24-35; Jesus' death and resurrection and the Church's mission, 26-28).
See E. Charpentier, *Lecture de l'évangile selon saint Matthieu [Reading the Gospel According to Saint Matthew]*, Paris 1974, p. 20.
5 See J. Zumstein, *Matthieu le théologien [Matthew the theologian]*, Paris, 1987, p. 46.

7

The gospel of Luke
and the Acts of the Apostles

Luke's originality lies in his being the author of two works which we might perhaps even consider one two-part work. He added another book to his gospel. In it he shows how the gospel, as a work of the Spirit, is not limited to the place of the Easter event, but that a wind blows out from Jerusalem which will bring it to the far ends of the earth. We know this book as the 'Acts of the Apostles'. The very fact that Luke even thought of writing a continuation to his gospel sheds an important light on his theological views, more specifically on his view of history as the place where God is revealed.

THE GOSPEL OF LUKE

Author, place and date of composition

Since the middle of the second century it has been generally accepted that the *author* of the third gospel and Acts is Luke, the physician (Col 4:14; see also Philem 24 and 2 Tim 4:11), who accompanied Paul on his second and third missions (see the so-called 'we' sections of Acts, i.e. parts written in the first person plural, Acts 16:10ff; 20:6ff; 27:1ff) and who later is also to have been with him for a time in Rome. Luke's gospel drew its authority in the Church largely from the fact that it was considered the work of a disciple of the great apostle.

There are very few exegetes who doubt that the third gospel and Acts were written by the same author. Even on the name

Luke (in Greek *Loukas*, a diminutive or variant of the name *Loukios/Lucius*) there is as such no reason for discussion. It is more difficult to decide whether this author may be considered Paul's travelling companion. In a still famous article Philip Vielhauer raised a storm in 1951 which has still not blown itself out. Many present day specialists in the Acts of the Apostles wonder whether the author of this book could even have known Paul.[1] His representation of Paul differs rather strongly from the picture we receive from Paul's own letters; he sometimes makes historical errors about Paul, his theology is not Pauline and he seems to be unfamiliar with Paul's letters, or at least seems not to have been inspired by them when portraying the apostle. On the other hand, none of these arguments are absolutely compelling, and the last one can even be used to defend his personal acquaintance with Paul. Historically, it is a difficult and complex point and we now have too little data – as is so often the case – to be able to provide a definitive answer. It remains a possibility that the author of the third gospel and Acts was one of Paul's companions – but then at most sporadically and for short periods. The balance in the modern literature about Acts tilts slightly in the direction of an otherwise unknown Christian.

Meanwhile, it is sure that the author is a *gentile Christian*, who grew up in a Greek cultural environment, but with a thorough knowledge of the Greek translation of the Bible then in circulation, the Septuagint, whose style and method of historiography he partially adopts. He must have been a cultured person and his writings betray a synthetic spirit and irenical temperament.

– As to the *place* where the third gospel was written, we can really only guess. Achaia (Greece) or Antioch have been suggested as have other places in Europe and the Near East. Perhaps the area around Antioch makes the best sense, but there is no compelling argument for this localization. Again the most important question seems to be: *for what audience did Luke write his gospel?*

We have no need to doubt that he wrote for gentile Christians. He provides adaptations for his non-Jewish public much more consistently than does Mark. Even the gospel's Palestinian-Jewish background begins to become somewhat vague in Luke; he omits for the most part discussions on specific Jewish problems and even replaces some Palestinian situations with others. Compare, for example, Lk 6:47-49 with Mt 7:24-27. Where Matthew speaks of a house built on a rock or on sand, Luke speaks of a house with or without an excavated foundation. Or compare Lk 5:19 with Mk 2:4. Where the bearers in Mark make a hole in the Palestinian flat roof made of a layer of beams filled in with branches and covered with a layer of lime, Luke speaks of removing the tiles usual for houses of a Roman type.

Luke has introduced his two writings with a small prologue from which it seems that he offers them to a certain Theophilus. Here he follows the custom of Hellenistic and Roman writers. We have no idea at all who this Theophilus may be. Was he an important person who had become a Christian? Or was he a gentile who wanted to learn something about Christianity? Was he Luke's patron? Very many guesses have been made and many identifications with well known figures from the period have been tried. This becomes easier in proportion to the paucity of the data. Some have even thought it may be a figure of style (Theo-philus – friend of God, would then be a symbolic name), which Luke uses to accommodate the more cultured readers of his gospel. Be it as it may (personally, we think Theophilus was a real person), it is not likely that Luke wrote his gospel as private reading matter for one person only. The very fact that we are in possession of the gospel at all pleads for a wider distribution of the writing.

As to the *date*, for a long time Luke's gospel was dated before 60. This came about primarily because it was thought that he had written the Acts of the Apostles before Paul's death (because of the Acts' 'open end') and the gospel even earlier. Given what we know now, it is not possible to retain this dating. First and foremost, there is the fact that Luke, just as Matthew, is dependent on Mark's gospel. Secondly, he reworked Mark's so-called parousia (or eschatological or apocalyptic) discourse (Mk 13) in a way which leaves little doubt that Luke already knew of the destruction of Jerusalem, see especially Lk 21:20-

21,24. The gospel was therefore in any case edited after the year 70. But it must have been written before Paul's letters were widely circulated making the years 80 to 90 the best approximation, about the same time as or somewhat later than Matthew's gospel. The Acts of the Apostles, whose place of origin is equally unknown, must then have been somewhat later, but may probably be dated within the same decade.

Luke as editor

Like Matthew, Luke is dependent on Mark and the *Quelle*. But he handles his sources *much more freely* than does Matthew. He is continually editing the traditional material at hand and his arrangement of this material is also on the whole more complex than Matthew's. While Matthew works more at compiling his sources (i.e. he uses Mark, Q and his *Sondergut* material fairly intactly, putting them together in one volume, as it were) Luke edits more fragmentarily taking now a piece of Mark, then a bit of *Quelle* adding some *Sondergut* here and there. He 'mixes' more than Matthew.

Where Matthew takes over Mark's gospel practically completely, Luke leaves out parts such as Mk 6:45-8:25; 10:1-12; 11:12-14,20-25; etc. Several motives could play a part in these *omissions*. Perhaps the author considered some passages unimportant or difficult for his gentile Christians to understand; perhaps he wanted to avoid repetition (the so-called doublets); perhaps there were reasons of literary and theological composition...

In addition to omissions, we also find a number of *transpositions* of Mark's material. Luke 'disturbs' the order of the triple tradition more seriously than does Matthew. As we noted when discussing the synoptic tradition (see above p. 107), Luke has five important transpositions of Mark's ordering. Matthew has more, but remarkably they are limited almost completely to the section Mk 1:21-6:13 = Mt 4:23-13:58.

≥ We find a good example of a (small) 'disturbance' of Mark's ordering in Lk 6:12-19 where he inverts the order of Mk

3:7-19. Mark tells first the *summarium* of the approaching crowds and then recounts the appointment of the twelve. Luke does just the reverse. This probably is done to create a suitable situation for including his 'sermon on the plain' which he copies from Q, a source that also provides the majority of the material for Matthew's sermon on the mount. Jesus chooses the twelve with whom he then descends to the plain where he addresses the crowd gathered there. Reversing Mark's ordering of 'the calling of the disciples – healing Peter's mother-in-law' (Mk 1:16-20,19-30 – Lk 4:38-39; 5:1-11 – see above p. 129 ff) may have a similar editorial reason. Luke creates a situation in which the future disciples have already seen that Jesus performs signs (4:38-39) and in which everyone was able to listen to his teaching (5:1-4). It thus becomes psychologically acceptable that they cast their nets at his command – here we have a symbolic story with a view to the later 'miraculous catch' of the gentile mission – and follow him when he calls. This last is of course an authentic historical recollection. Jesus did collect a group of followers around himself, and the whole story of the miraculous catch of fish can be a development of the – most likely – historical saying, 'I will make you fishers of men', that Matthew and Luke both retain from Mark's calling story. ≤

Luke's deviations with regard to Mark (and Matthew) are more numerous in the passion narrative, not so much due to transpositions in the sequence of the triple tradition as from the fact that Luke has much *Sondergut* in his passion narrative. This is so striking that a number of exegetes have offered the opinion that Luke must have used a source here other than Mark. Think, for example, of the well known passage where Jesus is sent from Pilate to Herod and back again (SgLk 23:6-12). This problem is even greater for the sources of John's gospel.

Of the three synoptic authors Luke has by and large the most *Sondergut*, 41% of his gospel. This *Sondergut* contributes greatly to the typical 'Lucan' distinction of the third gospel, especially because it contains many of his best known and best loved texts such as Zacchaeus, the prodigal son, the good Samaritan, Lazarus and the rich man, the travellers to Emmaus, etc. We cannot be sure where Luke found his *Sondergut*. We might think of oral tradition, separate recollections passed on within Luke's community, possibly also small written documents, and very probably also his own creativity on the basis of traditions (a sort of 'Lucan *midrash* technique'). In this way the Emmaus story can be a 'typical example' of the recognition of the Risen Lord, built on a combination of traditional appearance stories with the supper celebrations in the old Christian communities.

Luke has, more than the other evangelists, a concern to work as a real *historian*. He gives his writings a more 'scientific' allure. We see this in different things. In the style of the Hellenistic and Roman historiographers, he introduces his gospel with a prologue (1:1-4), where he dedicates his work, as it were, and where he sets out his purpose and work method. He also expressly wants to situate Jesus' history as an event in world history, within the *broader framework of the historical situation as it was then*. Read here, for example, Lk 2:1-2 and 3:1-2, where he even calls up the political constellation in Jesus' time. He also strives for *precision* and so replaces the title 'king' Herod in Mk 6:14 with the title 'tetrarch'. The 'sea of Galilee' (Mk 1:16) becomes, more correctly, a 'lake': see Lk 5:1 or 8:22,33. And finally Luke is the first one who dared to write a history of the primitive Church.

Paradoxically Luke's reputation as a scientific historian has served the interpretation of the gospels poorly. Luke was used as an argument to maintain that everything in the gospel and Acts was a hair-fine reconstruction of the facts. This meant that the evangelist's theological method was often overlooked and the gospels' truth was coupled too exclusively with their watertight historical exactness. But we must not be misled by Luke's more 'scientific' nature. It shows he is a cultured person with broad historical interests who was concerned with making his history of Jesus and the Church acceptable to the more educated reader. But this does not diminish the fact that for Luke, as for the other evangelists, the first concern is to tell about Jesus as a way to life. Luke is first of all *a believer and a theologian*, and only secondly an historian. Despite his prologue, his work (including Acts) is still much closer to the other evangelists' way of working and to *Old Testament historiography* (in which he is apparently quite proficient from his familiarity with the Septuagint), than to the profane historiography of the surrounding Greek and Roman world. Like the other evangelists, Luke has written no 'Life of Jesus' just as he has not written a 'Life of Paul' or a balanced report of the first months and years of the early Church. Like them, his work has a thesis. His intention is very clear, he wants to show in his gospel that Jesus is the Lord, and in Acts that the Spirit continues to work unstoppably.

As for his information, Luke, who was not a disciple from the first days, was dependent on his sources and on tradition. He has made undeniable historical errors, such as in Lk 2:1-5 where he associates Jesus' birth with the census ordered by Quirinius; or in Acts 9:20ff where he clearly contradicts the chronological order of events that Paul gives (compare Acts with Gal 1:15ff); or even in Acts 5:36-37 where he reverses the chronological places of Teudas and Judas the Galilean.

A fine example of Luke's 'theological' way of writing history can be found at the end of his gospel and at the beginning of the Acts, where he concentrates all events in Jerusalem. For Luke Jerusalem has an unusually important theological place. His gospel starts and finishes there. It is the place where everything relating to the Messiah takes place (is 'fulfilled'), the place where the Messiah entered into his glory (Lk 24:26) and from which the evangelization took flight to expand over the whole world to its very centre, i.e. Rome. There is a real parallelism between Jerusalem and Rome throughout Luke's two-part work. It is for this reason that Luke concentrates his story on Jerusalem. He makes the *journey to Jerusalem* a main theme of his gospel. Luke situates Jesus' most important sayings and the most important events around his person as well as the whole drama of the choice for or against Jesus during the journey to Jerusalem where Jesus, as Luke would have it, resolutely proceeds 'when the days drew near for him to be received up' (9:51). In Luke's gospel the journey to Jerusalem fills ten chapters! This representation, which deepens and expands Mark's portrait of the 'journeying Jesus' (see above p. 130), confers on Jesus the character of a travelling Christian missionary.

Moreover, even after the resurrection Luke concentrates everything in Jerusalem. Whereas in Mark and in Matthew Jesus orders his followers to go to Galilee (Mt 28:7,10,16ff, with Jesus' farewell apparently in Galilee; Mk 16:7), Luke omits all Galilean 'appearance traditions' and even has Jesus forbid his disciples to leave the city before Pentecost; see Lk 24:49; Acts 1:4. This allows him to develop his 'Jerusalem theology' (which leans heavily on the Old Testament). This will also be the reason why Luke wants to get Paul to Jerusalem as soon as possible after his conversion and why he has the initiative to carry a mission to the gentiles depend expressly on Peter's approval before Paul's missionary journeys (see Acts 9-13 where Paul's conversion comes first, followed by Peter's vision and the baptism of Cornelius under Peter's responsibility, and only then by the definitive start of Paul's activities among the gentiles). The real history of the first growth of the Christian communities was doubtless much more complex than Luke presents it.

We must also point out that Luke is by far the best writer of the four evangelists. He is an accomplished *stylist*, is well versed in the Greek language, has an integrated Hellenistic and biblical cultural background as well as having an evident gift for telling a good story, even if he is less picturesque and anecdotal than Mark. When he alters his sources, it is often to make stylistic or linguistic corrections. In some stories (think of the parable of the prodigal son) his qualities as story teller can match those of Andersen!

There is also a note on Luke's relationship to the Old Testament. As we said, his work shows a striking mastery of biblical style. Luke seems to be very familiar with the Greek version of the Old Testament then in general circulation, namely, the *Septuagint* translation (abbreviated LXX for its, by repute, seventy authors). In his gospel and Acts he makes a conscious effort to imitate this text. He leaves little doubt that he wants to follow in the path of the biblical historiographers. His quotations are taken exclusively from the Greek Bible, not the Hebrew or Aramaic (Targum) text traditions. Luke's familiarity with the Septuagint gives his own Greek an Old Testament flavour.[2]

Theological features of Luke's gospel

Jesus in Luke's gospel

– Like Matthew, Luke is dependent on Mark's theological outline since he has adopted Mark's framework and basic chronology. Nevertheless, we have the impression that Luke somewhat softens Mark's 'hard' crucifixion theology. Luke's Jesus is above all a Messiah who *is on the way to Jerusalem*, i.e., to the place where all the Old Testament promises will be fulfilled. For Luke, Jerusalem is no longer the symbol of unbelief and rejection as it is in Mark, but is the place of the ultimate messianic revelation.

≥ – Luke's portrait of Jesus has its very own distinction. His Jesus radiates mildness and mercy without in any way losing radicality or force. Luke prefers to show Jesus as the Redeemer of *those who do not belong*, the rejected or less respected, the poor, people who have been branded by society, the unclean, the sinners. See such *Sondergut* as 2:8-20 (the shepherds); 10:25-37; 17:11-19 (a Samaritan as example); 18:9-14 (a tax collector as example); 19:1-10 (Zacchaeus). We may situate Luke's attention for gentiles and women in the same line (see Luke's version of the healing of the centurion's servant, 7:1-10, as well as 8:1-3; 10:38-42; 23:27-31,55f).

– Luke's attention for *the poor and the deprived* is conspicuous and correlative to this are his harsh warnings and condemnations of greed and wealth. Read for example Lk 1:53; 4:18; 6:20-26 (much more biting than Matthew!); 12:13-21; 16:19-31. He also insists, more than the other evangelists, on the demand to leave everything behind when following Jesus. Read Lk 5:11 and compare it with Mt 4:20 and Mk 1:18; Lk 5:28 and compare it with Mt 9:9 and Mk 2:14. Read also Lk 14:25-33. It is striking how many of these texts belong to Luke's *Sondergut*. Luke displays particularly acute attention for material poverty and for the plague of greed.

– The *Sondergut* highlighting *Jesus' mercy for sinners* is also noticeably great. It is Jesus' mission 'to seek and to save the lost' (19:10). Read on this subject 7:36-50; the three parables in

Lk 15; 18:10-14; 19:1-10; 22:61; 23:34; 23:42-43. The majority of these texts are found only in Luke. Yet this does not mean we may misuse Luke to grasp a kind of 'cheap grace', or assume it does not matter how you live 'so long as you have faith'. Luke forges stronger ties than anyone else between forgiveness and *conversion*. See Lk 1:16; 5:32; 13:3,5; 15:7,10; 24:47. Even the prodigal son returns!

– Luke also has attention for Jesus *at prayer*. Much more than the other evangelists, he mentions that Jesus prays at important moments or before important decisions. We find Mk 1:35 in Lk 5:16 and Mk 14:32-42 in Lk 22:40-46, but Lk 3:21 (at the baptism), 6:12 (when appointing the apostles), 9:18 (at Peter's confession of faith), 9:28 (at the transfiguration), 11:1 (at the Lord's Prayer) and 23:34,46 (on the cross) are unique to Luke.

– The role of the *Holy Spirit* in Jesus' life – the Spirit which Luke understands very much in its Old Testament sense of the creating, recreating and driving force of God himself – receives more pronounced attention in Luke than in Matthew and Mark. See 1:35 where the Holy Spirit (specified as 'the power of the Most High') is confessed to be the source of Jesus' very human historical existence; 4:14 (cp Mt 4:12 and Mk 1:14); 10:21 (cp Mt 11:25); 11:13 (cp Mt 7:11). ≤

A theology of history

Many exegetes and theologians are convinced that Luke's most important original contribution to New Testament theology must be sought in his view of history.

To understand this properly we must be aware that early Christianity was developed in an atmosphere of tense eschatological and apocalyptic expectation, an anticipation of the final day, of the definitive breakthrough of God's dominion and the judgement of the wicked. Traditionally the Jewish understanding of the Messiah was linked to the expectation of the end of time. When the Messiah came and God's dominion was definitively established, history ('this age') would in some way or another come to an end. The 'last days' would arrive.

The Christians also felt this anticipation. The glorified Lord would return to judge the world and his return was expected immanently. (This expectation that the Lord would return at the end of time is called the 'parousia expectation'.) Traces of this immanent eschatological event are found not only in the gospels (see e.g. Mt 10:23; many exegetes think Jesus himself shared these expectations of the end. Albert Schweizer even made them the key to his interpretation of Jesus). They are also spread throughout the letters in the New Testament. Paul also awaits – at least in the beginning – the Lord's speedy return (the parousia). See, for example, 1 Thess 4:15-17. In the second letter of Peter – dating from early in the second century – we still hear echoes of people who ridicule the Christians' immanent parousia, see 2 Pet 3:3-4.

Thus for the early Christians the *last days* had begun with the Lord's resurrection and glorification. This explains much of why the gospels attributed such importance to Jesus' apocalyptic discourse. It is also an additional reason why the early Christians were not interested in writing a biography or history of Jesus as such. One does not write a biography or memoirs when the end of the world is knocking on the door! By the time Luke wrote, the delay in the return must have become a growing problem for a number of Christians. Many had already died, most of the first witnesses had disappeared... Were they really correct in their proclamation? Would the Lord be long in coming? For when should the parousia really be expected?

Luke's work is an implicit answer to this problem. He will not only add to his gospel the first 'Church history' with a very open ending (read Acts 28:29-31) thereby implying that the spreading of the gospel is by no means finished, but he will also play down the tense eschatological climate in his gospel.

For Luke, Jesus no longer stands at the end of time but, as the German exegete Hans Conzelmann expressed it in a now famous book, he is *'the centre of time'*. We could, with Luke in hand, divide history, as it were, in three parts: the *time of preparation* and promise (time of the Old Testament), the *time of Jesus* who is the centre of time' and *the time of the Church* which now filled with the power of the Holy Spirit must carry the gospel further and 'witness' (a very important concept for Luke) to Christ to the end.

≥ Several editorial elements in the gospel point in this direction. We see that Luke omits the saying in Mk 1:15, 'The time is fulfilled and the kingdom of God is at hand' (compare Lk 4:14 with Mk 1:14f and Mt 4:17). He does the same with Jesus' saying on the day and the hour of the end. Read here Lk 21:29-33 and compare it with Mt 24:32-36 and Mk 13:28-29. The comment 'he is near, at the very gate' (Mk 13:29) is included in Matthew but omitted by Luke. Luke also drops Mk 13:32 while Matthew preserves it. In this and other ways Luke has removed the tense expectation of an immanent end from the whole of Mark's 'apocalyptic discourse'. Compare Lk 21:8-14 with Mk 13:5-20. For Luke the persecutions are no longer a sign of the end but events which 'must first take place' (21:12) 'until the time of the gentiles are fulfilled' (21:24). The parable of the ten pounds is also typical of Luke's view (Lk 19:11-28). While the parallel text in Matthew about the ten talents is put immediately before the last judgment and thus, as the parable of the wise and silly bridesmaids, clearly introduces the end (read Mt 24:37-25:46; the parable of the talents = Mt 25:14-30), Luke says expressly that Jesus tells this parable *to correct* the people 'because they supposed that the kingdom of God was to appear immediately' (Lk 19:11). ≤

The same perspective is continued in the beginning of Acts. The disciples' question as to the time when the kingdom will be established is put aside as irrelevant. Jesus rather points out their task in the world's salvation history. They are to be witnesses to the ends of the earth. This is also the sense of the angels' words at the ascension, 'why do you stand looking into heaven? This Jesus, who was taken up from you into heaven, will come in the same way...' – implying that they must first go out and fulfil the task assigned to them. See Acts 1:6-11.

We could think that the three-part division of time contradicts the 'promise – fulfilment' design of salvation history, but it only appears so. Luke has developed his altered experience of time within this design: The Old Testament promises have been fulfilled in Jesus (in Jerusalem) and the time of the Church

(which starts from Jerusalem) is the time in which this fulfilment will fructify the world. With his 'solution' to the parousia
problem, Luke has not abandoned the expectation of the end.
P. van den Berghe correctly writes, 'Luke has neither abandoned nor totally replaced the expectation of the end, but the
eschatological expectation has lost its urgent character and the
lasting present of daily history becomes more emphatically un-
derlined as a time of salvation. This is the blessed time of the
world's evangelization, of the Word's progress, of the witnesses, of the Church.' Getting nervous about the questions of
when the end will come or whether disasters and persecutions
are omens of an immanent 'end of the world', no longer has
meaning for Luke. The Church has better things to do.

THE ACTS OF THE APOSTLES

General purpose

To see how smoothly the Acts of the Apostles continues the
perspective of the third gospel, it is sufficient to compare the
end of the gospel (Lk 24:44-53) with the beginning of Acts
(Acts 1:4-11). The gospel flows over, as it were, into the Acts.
We may well consider this book as the continuation of Luke's
gospel at least in terms of organization and purpose. It is Luke's
intention to show that *Jesus' mission continues in the mission of
the Church.* The fulfilment of the promises of salvation in Jesus'
passion and death in Jerusalem does not mean the end, and his
glorification (ascension) does not mean the proclamation of his
immediate return with the accompanying judgement. All that
has happened since Jesus' ascension into heaven is just as much
a part of God's plan of salvation as everything that preceded it.
After the time of the prophets and the Scriptures and after the
time of Jesus' mission on earth, it is now the time of the
Church's mission, namely, to witness to the fulfilling of God's

salvation throughout history, and to carry the gospel to all peoples. God's Holy Spirit who inspired the prophets and who filled Jesus' life drives the Church irrepressibly throughout the world. The Acts of the Apostles have correctly been called 'the gospel of the Holy Spirit'.

The 'programme' of Acts is clearly represented at the beginning of the book. Read Acts 1:1-11, before Jesus was taken from them, he gave the apostles his *commission*. To carry out this commission they will be baptized with (be submerged in) the *Holy Spirit*. They need not be concerned about the time when the kingdom will be 'restored', but... 'you shall receive the power when the Holy Spirit has come upon you; and you shall be my witnesses in Jerusalem and in all Judea and Samaria and to the ends of the earth' (Acts 1:8). A commission from the Lord – the power of the Holy Spirit – being witness, these what Acts all about. And indeed, what immediately follows illustrates the book's programme. The group of witnesses is completed (there must be 12 since they are the basis of the Israel of the fulfilment as the patriarchs were the basis of the Israel of the promise); at Pentecost – the feast where in those days the Jews celebrated receiving the *Torah*! – they were baptized in the Holy Spirit. And immediately they began to do as Jesus had ordered to give witness in Jerusalem. The whole purpose of the rest of the book will be to illustrate the clause in 1:8: in Judea, in Samaria, and *to the ends of the earth*.

When Paul arrives in Rome at the end of the book, the purpose of Acts is complete. Rome was the centre of the then known world ruling 'to the ends of the earth'. The gospel had reached the capital of the world and could prosper there and continue to spread further. That is why Luke's writings may have an 'open' ending. The spread of the gospel did not finish with Paul's arrival in Rome. Rome is itself a new beginning for the Holy Spirit's work in history.

Structurally, the book of Acts has two main divisions.

1. A first part describes the Church's growth in Jerusalem with the first persecutions and the expansion into Judea, Samaria and beyond the borders of Palestine. The most important individual figures in this growth and expansion of 'the Way' are

Peter and the deacon Philip. Peter also opens the door for mission activity among the gentiles and takes an important step in this direction in baptizing the centurion Cornelius of Caesarea. This first part covers chapters 1-12.

2. The second part is wholly focused on the fate of the apostle Paul. A preview of this is present in the first part, where in Acts 7:58-8:1 he enters the scene as persecutor. In chapter 9, we read the story of Paul's sudden conversion just at the moment when he was most active in persecuting, the story of his inclusion in the Church in Damascus and his recognition as a Christian and an apostle in Jerusalem. Chapter 12 concludes with an account of Paul's activities in Antioch (with Barnabas and Mark). Starting with chapter 13, Paul definitively occupies the centre stage from where we will follow him on his three great missionary journeys and his transfer to Rome in chains. The second part of Acts covers chapters 13-28. This clearly shows that Paul is far and away the most important figure in Acts. When all is said and done, the traditional title of the book, 'The Acts of the Apostles' (a title which does not come from Luke) is somewhat misleading. Of the twelve we hear only of Peter (and a little of John).

That Paul is the focus of Acts teaches us something about the book's intention. We may accept that Acts was written between the years 85-90 for an audience of gentile Christians, most likely the same public for whom Luke's gospel was written.[3] These Christians, all of whom are in a certain way Paul's children (he was known as the apostle to the gentiles), experienced great difficulties in that period and mostly likely had questions about their place in the Church and in God's plan of salvation. The separation from Judaism – which had begun when the converts were no longer required to undergo circumcision and to live according to the Law of Moses – must have made many of them wonder whether they were on the right path.

We may therefore presuppose that the book of Acts was also written with the purpose of *explaining to Luke's contemporaries in his Church their situation and their vocation as Christians.* As Robert Maddox writes:

The Christians are the heirs of the promises made by God to the Hebrew patriarchs about a coming time of salvation – heirs who have entered into their inheritance. Those promises were made by God to the Hebrew national community, and were in the first instance fulfilled with Israel when God sent Jesus as Jewish messiah and saviour. But he intended, through Israel, to open up salvation to 'all flesh'. God's plan involved salvation for those who accepted it and judgement for those who rejected it. As things have turned out, it is largely gentiles who have accepted the offered salvation and Judaism which has rejected it. Therefore, surprisingly, Judaism has been judged by God. The substantial exclusion of Judaism from the fulfilment of its own ancestral promises does not however invalidate the promises themselves, or the fulfilment of the promises for those people, mainly gentiles, who have accepted them.[4]

Texts such as Acts 7:1-53 and 13:14-52 (especially vv. 46-48) illustrate the book's purpose as we have described it. Luke most likely feels compelled to emphasize this point because a number of Christians from his generation may have tended to think the opposite – especially after the year 70 when relations between Jews and Christians petrified and the Christians were excluded by the Pharisee synod at Jamnia (we referred to this above p. 138 f when discussing Matthew's gospel). Paul is doubtless a black sheep in the eyes of many 'Law'-abiding Jews, and many Christians also felt that Paul had led the good news down the wrong path. That is why Luke – who is really a very Pauline thinker when it comes to the mission to the gentiles and the universality of the Church – wants to demonstrate with the Acts of the Apostles (and in fact with his entire work) first of all, that Jesus is indeed the Messiah (gospel + Acts 1-2); secondly, that everything that had happened in the Church's development up to that moment has occurred under God's guidance, i.e. through the Holy Spirit; thirdly, that Paul did not betray the gospel but was rather the providential proclaimer of the faith Jesus himself desired. It is for this reason that Luke repeats three times the story of Paul's vocation and mission (Acts 9:1-19; 22:1-21; 26:9-18), where verses such as 22:18,21 and particularly 26:16-18 speak volumes. The tendency of these conversion stories puts into words very well Paul's own conviction, as he wrote of it in the letter to the Galatians, that his gospel does not derive from other people but from Christ himself and that God has chosen him to proclaim the gospel to the gentiles. Read Gal 1:11-16.

Theology and history

What we wrote earlier about Luke's theology of history in the third gospel is true also, of course, for the book of Acts (see above p. ff). We will therefore limit ourselves here to a few other aspects of the relationship between theology and history.

The general intention of Acts gives us a key to discover its own level of truth and as well as the relationship between the message of faith and historical information. The importance of this for a correct reading of Acts should not be underestimated, since the book's real message has suffered even more than the gospel from Luke's 'scientific' reputation.

Luke's stance as historian in Acts is no different than what is in his gospel. Even though the book of Acts looks much more like a history book than the gospel does, its ultimate purpose – and thus also its level of truth – is the same as the gospel's. *When writing Acts Luke is still an evangelist!* He is not writing neutrally informative history, but history in the service of the good news, of the confession of faith. Just as we need not be able to say after reading the gospel, 'Now I know exactly what happened in Jesus' life', but rather, 'Yes, Jesus is really the Messiah' (see above p. 160), so with Acts we must not conclude with the thought, 'Now I know the history of the early Church', but rather, 'Yes, the Holy Spirit of God has indeed been at work here'. *This* is what Acts is all about.

Of course, Acts contains information of inestimable historical value for our knowledge of the primitive Church and of Paul's activities in it. But as with the gospel, Acts does not pretend to deliver an exact or complete reconstruction of the facts. The purely historical value of Luke's story depends for the most part on his sources. Luke does not write as an eye-witness, unless – perhaps – in a few passages about Paul, but he has consulted sources. In the prologue to his gospel he writes that he has 'followed all things closely for some time past' and we need not doubt his serious and historical honesty. But we may not forget that the fact that Luke examined his sources closely does not automatically guarantee their absolute histori-cal exactness. We know what important sources he used for his gospel, Mark and the *Quelle*. We also know fairly well how he worked with these sources. Our information about Acts is not so extensive, but he certainly did have sources on the Church in Jerusalem, on the Church in Antioch, on Paul, etc. According to the author Gottfried Schille, examples of possible sources are lists of apostles and their helpers, stories about what the apostles did, stories about geographical areas, legends about the apos-tles, liturgical texts, local recollections, traditions about the preaching and the like.[5] Whatever sources he used or whatever recollection he drew upon, we need not doubt that Luke con-sulted his material with the eye of a believing theologian, of an evangelist who wanted to pass on a religious message. There is much evidence for this in Acts. A few examples as illustration:

– The book of Acts offers *no complete picture* of the early Church. We hear nothing of the missionary activity in Egypt which had begun very early and which was very important, nor do we hear of the very early establishment of a community in Rome (Paul did not found a community there!). The structure of Luke's book is really quite simple having the two main parts we described above (pp. 165-166). This structure implies a simpli-fication of the material and the perspective. In a manner of speaking the spotlights are reserved for Peter and Paul not the other apostles. The well-rounded continuous construction of the report abut Paul's missionary journeys can be somewhat decep-tive. For example, using Acts we can follow Paul on two trips to Corinth, the first when the community was founded, Acts 18, the second during the third missionary journey, Acts 20:2-3. But Paul himself twice writes to the Corinthians, 'Here for the *third* time I am ready to come to you' (2 Cor 12:14; 13:1). We know next to nothing of what the rest of the apostles did.

≥ – The incomplete picture is not only due to a lack of information. Luke *selects* his material very carefully to have it serve his theological plan. Here we return to what we wrote above (p. 158 f) about his Jerusalem theology. Does it not say something that he omits all references to appearances of the risen Lord in Galilee from both his gospel and Acts? See Mt 28:7,10,16-20; Mk 16:7; Jn 21. In Luke Jesus even *forbids* his disciples to leave the city of Jerusalem. This can only be explained from the author's theological intention. He wants to make Jerusalem the exclusive centre from which everything begins. The city of the promises, of the fulfilment as the city of Easter, is also the city from which the gospel was spread. In other words, Luke imposes a type of centralization which historically speaking is without doubt an incorrect simplification. The birth and growth of the early Church was much more complex than Luke's description suggests. ≤

– Luke *idealizes* his picture of the early Church. The well known description of life in the community in Jerusalem (Acts 2:42-47 and 4:32-36) is an idealized generalization which is even contradicted in Acts itself by texts such as 6:1. The Christians' first euphoria doubtless brought with it examples of people who disposed of all their worldly goods, but Luke idealizes this to a general picture because he wants to hold up the first community in Jerusalem for emulation as a pure example of evangelical life. In other words, in this description there is a stimulating and cautionary (parenetical – from *parenesis,* meaning exhortation, advice) purpose toward his own Christians.

This idealization also plays a role in the picture Luke gives of Peter and Paul. It is evident that the picture we meet here is already coloured by the deep respect the Church has for these two apostles. We find ourselves at the gates of Christian hagio-graphy here. Peter's role regarding the mission to the gentiles is simplified, and everyone who has read Paul's letters knows that the impressions they give of the apostle to the gentiles can often differ from the portrait drawn in Acts. We should also note that the chronology of Paul's life in Acts does not always agree with what can be deduced from the letters. Here too Luke could have simplified or restructured a number of data for theological reasons.

– As in his gospel, Luke remains in the Acts much closer to the biblical (Old Testament) style of writing history than to the Hellenistic or Roman style. Acts belongs much more to the so-called 'historical narrative' (such as is found in the books of Samuel) than to 'scientific' historiography. It is striking just how *anecdotal* Luke's writing is. Many elements which an historian would absolutely exert every effort to discover and report seem not to interest him at all, such as main developments, dates, etc. We know, for example, that Paul spent at least two years in Ephesus, that he did important work to establish the community there, that he experienced difficulties and landed in prison. Every historian would like nothing better than to know in what surroundings and under what circumstances he worked there; what contacts he maintained, while there, with other Churches; what his relations were with the Johannine community established in that city, etc. Luke's report on Ephesus is as good as limited to two anecdotes in Acts 19. A close examination shows that the anecdotal approach to history serves a theological purpose. Nearly all the stories Luke tells are supposed to illustrate how unstoppable is God's work done through his missionaries, despite all opposition and persecution.

We find another aspect of the 'biblical' style of writing in the *miraculous atmosphere* surrounding the book of Acts. The book bubbles over with miracles and miraculous events. There are three stories on miraculous escapes from prison alone (Acts 5:18-23; 12:3-12; 16:23-30). It is more than evident that what we have here is a legendary genre. Many people have already noted that the atmosphere surrounding Acts contrasts strongly with the sobriety of Paul's letters where we learn nearly nothing of all the wondrous events the apostle is to have met with. Luke's models are the Old Testament and the gospels! The miracle stories (in which, as in the gospel, history and legend have become intertwined) want to illustrate the presence of God's hand in everything that happens to the apostles. In a certain sense they have the same function as the repeated references to the Holy Spirit in events and decisions.

– Finally, a word about the numerous *speeches* in the book of Acts. There are different types of speeches such as 'mission speeches' to Jews and gentiles (2:14-41; 3:12-26; 4:9-12; 13:16-41; 17:22-31, etc.); 'apologetic speeches' (22:1-21; 26:2-24), Paul's valedictory speech to Miletus (20:18-35); Stephen's speech (7:1-53); Peter's speech (11:4-18) and still more. Noteworthy here is that all these speeches have the same style and tendency. All the speakers speak like Luke! These speeches were not transcribed from stenographer's notes made at the time of delivery, but were composed for the most part by Luke himself even though, for the mission speeches, he referred back to real data from the time of the early Church history.

We can conclude that in the book of Acts, Luke has given us a splendid complement to his gospel. The book offers extremely interesting historical information on the early Church, but we may not forget that this information is selected and stylized. Like the gospels, Acts of the Apostles is above all a book of faith. If we read it as such we will profit the most from it.

NOTES

1   P. Vielhauer, 'Zum Paulinismus der Apostelgeschichte' [On the Paulinism of Acts] in *Evangelische Theologie* X (1950-51), pp. 1-15. Since this article many authorities answer negatively to the question as to whether Luke was Paul's companion, among them E. Haenchen, G. Schneider, E. Plümacher, A. Weiser. Others, such as J. Fitzmeyer, continue to presuppose a positive answer is still possible.

2   It is important to know this for a correct appreciation of a number of Luke's stories or expressions. The meaning of a number of words must not be sought first of all in how they are used in classical Greek texts, but in how the Septuagint uses them to translate Hebrew concepts.

3   As we said when introducing the gospel, the place of origin is uncertain. Antioch, Achaia (Greece), Asia (Ephesus) and Rome have all been suggested.

4   R. Maddox, *The Purpose of Luke-Acts*, FRLANT 126, Göttingen: Vandenhoeck & Ruprecht, 1982, p. 183.

5   G. Schille, *Anfänge der Kirche, Erwägungen zur apostolischen Frühgeschichte* [*The Church's Beginnings, Attempts at an Ancient History of the Apostles*], München, 1966, 238 pp. Idem, *Die Apostelgeschichte des Lukas* [*Luke's Acts of the Apostles*], ThHKNT 5, Berlin, 1983, 482 pp.

The gospel of John

The gospel of John and the synoptic authors

In a class of its own

'In the beginning was the Word, and the Word was with God, and the Word was God...' From the very opening of John's gospel we are given the impression that we have entered another world from that of the synoptic authors. A majestic hymn open the portals to a gospel which in many ways is *in a class of its own*. We will start by listing a few important 'eye-catchers' which illustrate this.

≥ 1. The geography and chronology of John's gospel diverges on numerous points from that of the synoptics. Only John seems to know of Jesus' activity in Judea (including calling the disciples) before John the Baptist was taken prisoner and, what is more, after a first period of activity in Galilee John situates one in Jerusalem (Jn 1:19-3:36).

– In John's gospel the centre of gravity of Jesus' activity is Judea and Jerusalem. Galilee is less important. Jesus is there only in John 2:1-12; 4:43-54 (both times in Cana); 6:1-7:9. In the synoptics it is clearly different, since there Jesus is in Jerusalem for only the last few weeks of his life.

– John mentions several journeys to Jerusalem (2:13; 5:1; 7:10; 12:12?); the synoptics mention only one.

– John refers to Jesus' presence in Jerusalem during at least three passover feasts (2:13; 6:4; 11:55). According to this chronology Jesus' public life must have filled a good two years (tradition says three years) while in the synoptics it seems to have taken less than one. ≤

It is tempting to take the easy way out and explain the

difference between John and the synoptics exclusively with an 'addition' or 'correction' theory, as if John (in the position of Jesus' most beloved disciple) is to have completed and/or corrected the data of Matthew, Mark and Luke with his own recollections. On many points the geographical and chronological framework of John's gospel can just not be reconciled with that in the synoptics, just as we cannot merge the infancy narratives found in Matthew and Luke. The question whether John's gospel presupposes that its readers know the synoptics (which we would have to accept if we were to have John's gospel complete or correct them) is far from solved, even though it is an important and interesting subject of discussion among exegetes today. We may not forget that the concern to make John corroborate the synoptics in the areas of historical reporting originally grew from a desire to make the four gospels, cost what it may, agree as a report of Jesus' words and deeds. If John has corrected the synoptics on some points, then we will have to concede that they had been in error on these points – but then we would also wonder whether John was always correct? Again, beside being an impossible task, making the four gospels agree in terms of historicity is, as we have seen in the previous chapters, an outmoded problem.

≥ 2. As substantial as the problems relating to the framework, are John's differences with the synoptics in terms of *narrative material and saying material*. As far as narrative material is concerned, outside of the passion narrative where of course the same events are related – but where John does not really adopt even one pericope from the synoptics and this as of theLast Supper – *the narrative material common to all of them is limited to five pericopes* (2:13-16; 6:1-13; 6:16-21; 12:1-8; 12:12-19). Of the 29 miracles in the synoptics, only two are mentioned in John, the multiplication of the loaves (6:1-13) and the walking on water (6:16-21). On the other hand he relates fivemiracles which appear to be extremely important in Jesus' activity, which make us wonder why we do not find them in the synoptics, namely, the wedding at Cana (2:1-11); the healing of the son of the royal functionary (4:46-54; our opinion is that this is a variant on the healing of the centurion's servant found in Mat-

174

thew and Luke); the healing of the paralytic in Jerusalem (5); the healing of one born blind (9) and the raising of Lazarus (11). The last three miracles are presented as extremely important for explaining the authorities' antagonistic attitude toward Jesus. They are even thought to be the causes of his persecution and death, another reason to be surprised at their absence in the synoptics. The difficulty cannot be solved by saying that John only wanted to report miracles which the synoptics missed. This does not explain *why* the synoptics, who have many more miracle stories than John, missed just such important miracles, even less why John then does include the multiplication of the loaves and the walking on water. Healings of the possessed are completely absent in John; the cleansing of the temple (2:13-16) and Jesus' anointing (12:1-8) are given other places in his gospel than the ones they have in the synoptics. ≤

– In the *sayings material* the differences are equally evident. John's gospel contains more sayings material (words of Jesus) than do the synoptics. Chapters 3 to 17 contain almost exclusively speeches, monologues, dialogues and controversies, or better, expanded discussions. But none of these great speeches from Jesus are found in the synoptics (not even the long speech at the multiplication of the loaves – which event they do mention – nor the so important and comprehensive farewell discourse at the Last Supper). The *thematic content* of the sayings material in John also differs considerably from that of the first three gospels. The 'kingdom of God' (kingdom of heaven) which in the synoptics is the focal point of Jesus' preaching is mentioned in John only in the conversation with Nicodemus (3:3,5) which is absent in the synoptics. The absence of this concept in John is even more remarkable when we think that all historians of the New Testament agree that the proclamation of the kingdom of God was *historically* central to Jesus' activity.

In John's gospel the main themes are: Life, Light and Truth (and their opposites). In John's controversies the disputed issue is no longer Jesus' observance of the Law (fasting, marriage, keeping the Sabbath, etc.) but practically only faith in Jesus as the one sent by the Father. Life or judgement depends on that belief. Separate moral prescriptions are also absent from John's gospel, where Jesus summarizes all commandments in this one, to love one another as Jesus loved his own.

The real parables, so typical of Jesus' way of teaching are also unknown in John's gospel. Is it not strange that someone who must have known Jesus so well reflects none of the synoptic parables? The closest John comes to parables are 'I sayings' (I am the door to the sheep, I am the good shepherd, the door, the way, the truth and the life). See above pp. 69-70.

3. The *image of Jesus* is also very different from what is found in the synoptics. His way of speaking is much less graphic than in the synoptics. He speaks a formal, doctrinal, abstract, poetically liturgical and often very difficult language. His whole figure is surrounded with a sort of mysterious halo generally absent in the synoptics (which has contributed to the popularity of John's gospel among esoteric sects). It is the already glorified Son of God who speaks. This is particularly evident in the passion narrative. On this Donatien Mollat has written:

> Jesus is aware of all that will happen to him (18:4), he controls the events and the people (18:4-8; 19:11). His agony in the Garden of Gethsemani is not mentioned, nor is his cry of abandonment on the cross [but the confirmation of his completed mission is]. He is the master of his last moments and gives up his life with the full awareness and grandeur of a presiding priest (19:28-30). His life is not taken, he gives it (10:18).[1]

But still a real gospel

The penetrating differences between John's gospel and the synoptics do not justify concluding that John has not written a real gospel. The differences move on an undercurrent of similarities.

– John's gospel is also a *story about Jesus*, about his words and deeds, about his conflict with the representatives of official Judaism, about his death and resurrection.

176

– The story begins with John the Baptist, takes place in Galilee and Judea, and ends in Jerusalem.

– We can divide the material into narrative material and saying material.

– We find miracles, controversies, comparisons, a passion narrative and also a number of themes met in the synoptics. Despite 'being in a class of its own', John's gospel rests on an historical background similar to that of the other gospels. This *concordia discors* between John and the synoptics is a much discussed point in modern research. It is an important problem in the question of the relationship between the fourth gospel and the synoptics. If it is true that the basic structure of our present gospels is the result of the assembling of separate traditions (by Mark?), then it must be asked whether John, who integrates the same basic elements in his gospel, may not have learned of the gospel structure from Mark or another of the synoptics...

– Especially in his plan and purpose, John demonstrates that it is a fully fledged gospel. John's story about Jesus is anything but neutrally informative, rather it *testifies and calls to faith*. In this sense it shares completely the concern of the other gospels and must be read with the same key to interpretation. It must be read as a book written from faith and wanting to proclaim the truth of salvation. That John's theological accents and points of view differ from those of the synoptics does not diminish this fundamental agreement in their purpose. A. Lemmers puts it this way,

> The gospel of John is presented as a gospel, i.e. as the proclamation of Jesus' words and deeds as a message bringing salvation and summoning to faith. This proclamation, as it is expressed in the gospels, is not in the first place interested in historically accurate reporting of facts which took place in an accurately determinable period of time with regard to one Jesus of Nazareth, but rather in *the meaning* Jesus of Nazareth's life, death and resurrection have *for salvation*. This is true for all the canonical gospels, and John's gospel is only the ripest fruit of this written gospel

production and the perfect incarnation of what a gospel really wants to be.[2]

The purpose of John's gospel is magnificently expressed in its original conclusion, 'Now Jesus did many other signs in the presence of the disciples, which are not written in this book; but these are written *that you may believe that Jesus is the Christ, the Son of God, and that believing you may have life in his name*' (Jn 20:30f).

John and the synoptics

It is not difficult to imagine that many questions have arisen on John's relationship to the synoptics. Did the author of John's gospel – given the striking uniqueness of this book – work completely independently? As long as there was no problem in thinking that the apostle John, as a disciple who had experienced all these things, had written his own eye-witness report enriched by years of profound meditation, this independence caused no great difficulties. According to the traditional view, all four of the evangelists had worked independently. John's position in tradition as Jesus' beloved disciple conferred on him a privileged position. It was generally thought that John had known of the other three gospels but that after many years of meditation on the mystery of Christ, he composed his own gospel as a correction and completion, i.e. he related primarily the words and signs of Jesus which the synoptics, for whatever reason, overlooked or omitted, and which had taken place for the most part in Jerusalem. But it is clear that this traditional view had lost sight of the striking differences in the style of Jesus' words (Jesus speaks in John's gospel in the same style found in the first letter of John!), while it was also unable to explain satisfactorily the already mentioned absence of the whole farewell discourse or the raising of Lazarus from the synoptics.

With what we now know of the growth of the gospel traditions, the lay of the land has changed. Did John, independent of Mark or the other synoptic authors, also put the separate bits of traditional material available to him (material very different from what was available to the synoptic authors) in a narrative framework? And must he also, like Mark, be considered an independent creator of the gospel genre? Or did he, rather, know Mark (and possibly the other gospels) and become inspired by the synoptic gospel structure to compose his own work? Did he only know the synoptics or did he also use them? Did he, indeed, consciously complete and correct? Texts such as Jn 3:22-24 have been referred to in this context. There the evangelist tells how Jesus also baptized in Judea beside John the Baptist. In verse 24 we read of the Baptist, 'For John had not yet been put in prison'. From John's gospel alone we see no direct reason why this comment should be made, since it seems to presuppose the reader might think that John has already been taken prisoner. The text gives the impression of being a correction. Several exegetes have offered the opinion that Jn 3:24 could be an implicit correction of the synoptics' presentation, according to which Jesus only began his public life *after* John had been taken prisoner. There are also those who believe they see a correction of the synoptics in Jn 19:17 – bearing his own cross – where the synoptics differ in saying that Simon of Cyrene helped carry the cross (see Mk 15:21; cf above p. 21).

All these questions gain in importance when we realize that John's gospel in all likelihood was written later than Matthew's or Luke's and also probably in a flourishing community where there was a real chance of knowing Mark's gospel (and perhaps the other synoptics, especially Luke).

The question of John's relationship to the synoptics is of course very closely tied to the question of the fourth gospel's *sources*. Did John have his own sources? (Oral traditions? Texts? The preaching of an apostle?) Especially for his miracle stories and for his passion narrative it is thought he may have had *separate written sources*. The famous German exegete and theologian Rudolf Bultmann believed that John's miracle stories came from a 'sign source'' (the technical name for it is *Ssemeia-Quelle;* John always refers to Jesus' miracles as *Semeia*, i.e. 'signs'). It has also been suggested that John had separate sources for Jesus' discourses, for the Johannine passion narrative and for the appearance stories. The problem is extremely complex and there is as yet no unanimity among exegetes on the matter. As we said, traditional exegesis was convinced that John wanted to complete and correct the synoptics. Since 1938, when a British exegete, P. Gardner-Smith, published a study entitled *Saint John and the Synoptic Gospels*, a tendency has arisen to defend John's independence in the sense that John did *not* know the synoptics and thus made no attempts to complete or correct them. We can summarize the current state of affairs in the research as follows:

– The majority of the important modern specialists in the fourth gospel[3] share the opinion that the author of the gospel of John worked outside any literary dependence on the synoptic gospels. This, of course, explains why there are differences. The agreements between John and the synoptics (a good example is Jn 12:1-8 // Mk 14:3-9) must be explained from a common tradition. The picture given is on the whole that the original – Palestinian – tradition about Jesus became *subdivided before* it was committed to writing. The different branches more of less underwent their own evolution according to the preachers who used and spread them, or according to the communities where the traditions were preserved and passed on. Some of these traditions later formed the basis of Mark's gospel; another part became the *Quelle*, still other parts were probably responsible for Matthew's and Luke's *Sondergut* material. The branching of the Jesus tradition could also have led to different variants of the passion narrative... Continuing to reason in the same line a number of exegetes suggests that John's gospel is the *result of his own early branch of the Jesus tradition*. The apostle John and his communities could have been the ones to preserve and pass on this separate branch of tradition. Thus these exegetes explain the agreements between John and the synoptics on the basis of the common (historical, Palestinian) origin of the tradition. The uniqueness of the fourth gospel is explained by that tradition's early subdivision into branches plus, of course, the evangelist's own contribution which is larger than that of the synoptic authors.

As illustration of the independent tradition thesis we provide another simple diagram inspired by a book written by Stephen

Smalley, *John Evangelist and Interpreter*. From a Palestinian basic tradition the material developed which, on the one hand, would lead to the synoptic gospels (here we find the diagram of the two-source theory) and, on the other, to the fourth gospel, namely, John's own traditions, SgJn, plus what John has in common with the synoptics.

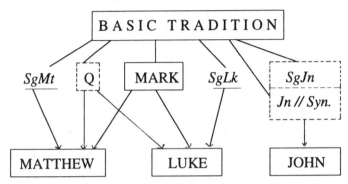

– For the past few years some exegetes have been defending the position that, on the contrary, John *was* literarily dependent on Mark for smaller or larger parts of his gospel.[4] Note carefully that this is not the same as a return to the traditional view of a John who completes and expands the synoptic material about Jesus; it is rather the gleanings of modern form criticism and redaction criticism. According to this theory John, like Matthew and Luke, would have derived his basic structure from Mark. But then – if the dependency theory is correct – he exercised his own personal and theological interest and a very great freedom in using his source, which explains how the huge difference came about. This position can at first seem strange, but nevertheless it can call up a good number of fundamental arguments is its favour. The discussions on this are of course held on a very technical level, so that we will have to be content here with a simple summary. A classic example of John's possible literary dependence on Mark can be found in Jn 12:3 // Mk 14:3. Both passages speak of 'ointment of *pistikos* nard'. Most translations render *pistikos* as 'pure'. But some authors think this means nard ointment made from the oil of *pistachio* nuts. The word *pistikos* is rare, and the fact that both Mark and John use it in the same place makes us think of the case of the word *pterugion* for the temple's pinnacle (see above p. 104). Such a peculiarity can be an argument in favour of the thesis that John knew Mark's text.

Those defending the thesis that John used Mark generally expend less effort in searching for separate sources which would have provided material for the gospel of John. They attribute the originality of the fourth gospel as compared to its predecessors more particularly in *the author's own editorial originality*. Without ourselves trying to find a definitive answer in this short summary, we must say that we are personally convinced that the reason for the originality of the fourth gospel is more to be sought in the editorial work of the evangelist than in unique historical data, sources or recollections which he is to have had available. In other words, we believe that the originality of the fourth gospel should be sought first of all in the writer and theologian John rather than in his sources.

This point is also important with regard to the question of the historical trustworthiness of the fourth gospel. The researchers who posit that John worked independently of the synoptics with separate sources for the tradition, will in general estimate his historical informative value highly. Those who think that John had no other sources to speak of than what Mark or the synoptics had and who attribute his differences to his editorial activity, will of course have a lesser appreciation of his historical accuracy of his information. We face here again an example of the complexity of the problems. The question of the historical accuracy of the gospels continually crosses paths with the problems of their mutual relationship and their sources. This means that historical criticism and literary criticism depend on one another, or at least continually have to take one another into consideration.

It is thus not true that we should deny John all historical trustworthiness. On the contrary, many exegetes are convinced – and we share the conviction – that the gospel of John gives on some points more trustworthy historical information than do the synoptics. Thus it is quite possible that Jesus went several times to Jerusalem and that his public life lasted longer than the structure of Mark's gospel suggests. It is also possible that Jesus was active for a time near John the Baptist before the latter was taken prisoner, and that the text of Jn 3:23-24 thus represents an accurate historical recollection. There could also be relevant historical recollections in the passion narrative. Moreover, the author of the fourth gospel appears to have a good knowledge of Jewish customs and of the topography of Jerusalem. Thus, we may certainly not deny the fourth gospel all informative value. But the historical exactness of the events – just as for all other biblical texts – must be tested against the principles of a healthy historical criticism. In this the gospel of John does not differ from other writings and it can make its own historical contribution. But it is equally clear that John considers providing historical information the least of his goals. More emphatically than the synoptics he treats the recollections about Jesus with great freedom in service of an exclusively theological symbolic interest. And in any case the question of his relationship to the synoptics – as we have already written – makes a judgement on his historical value an extremely complicated matter. It is as yet impossible to achieve unanimity or lucidity on this and other questions. For example, in the most recent edition of his commentary of the gospel of John, C. K. Barrett writes that his belief in the historical informative value of the fourth gospel is but very small, because John's interest obviously lies elsewhere and because of his creativity as a writer.

Author, place and date of origin

– Like the other gospels, the fourth gospel does not identify its *author*. We have testimony from the second century (among which from Irenaeus of Lyon) that the author is the apostle John, the son of Zebedee, who belonged to the first of Jesus' disciples. In later Church tradition, this identification was as good as undisputed. This view was believed to be firmly supported given the reference in Jn 21:24 to the beloved disciple, 'This is the disciple who is bearing witness to these things, and who has written these things; and we know that his testimony is true.' Nowhere is the 'beloved disciple' mentioned by name, but he has always been identified with the apostle John. For centuries Jn 21:24 was considered the evangelist's hidden signature.

But this verse is not so decisive as has long been thought. We now know from literary criticism that the 21st chapter of John has been added by a follower. The gospel originally ended with the 20th chapter, at the end of Jesus' appearance to Thomas.

The fourth gospel does indeed look like an eye-witness report (Jn 19:25; 20:24-29) of the 'beloved disciple' ('one of his disciples, whom Jesus loved' in 13:23; 19:26f; 20:2,4,8; 21:7), who may perhaps be equated with the unnamed disciple of 1:39 and 18:15. There is even a chance that with this disciple John the son of Zebedee and brother of Jacob is meant, although this question too brings great difficulties, such as, how would a simple fisherman from Galilee be someone known to the high priest, as is said in Jn 18:15? Typical for the evolution of opinions on this problem is the changed position of two of the most authoritative commentators on the gospel of John in our time, Rudolf Schnackenburg and Raymond Brown. In the first part of his voluminous commentary on the gospel of John published in 1965, Schnackenburg defended the identification of the beloved disciple with the apostle John. In the third part, published ten years later, he writes, 'The beloved disciple was certainly a disciple of the Lord, but was not one of the Twelve; most likely he was a resident of Jerusalem.' In the same way Brown, in his great commentary dating from 1966, defends the identification of the beloved disciple with John, but changed his opinion in a book published in 1979. With them a number of other authors share the opinion that the beloved disciple is not the apostle John but an otherwise unknown – and probably Jerusalemite – disciple of Jesus.[5]

And there is more. Even if the traditional identification of the beloved disciple with John the son of Zebedee should appear to be correct, this by no means proves that John was the material author of the book. This disciple is spoken of in the third person, and it must also be admitted that a reference to one's self as 'the (most) beloved of Jesus' disciples' can hardly be explained as a sign of great humility. It appears much more to be an 'honourary title' given him by others, namely, by a community which appealed to him and where he was held in great esteem. In 21:24 we read, 'who has written these things'. This expression can also be explained as meaning, 'who is the source of what is written here, to whom this writing appeals as authority'. We must also remain aware that in the Bible and in the Jewish literature of that time (the so-called intertestamental literature) the phenomenon of what is known as *pseudepigraphy* was far from unfamiliar. With this is meant a procedure where an anonymous writing was attributed to a well known or authoritative figure. In the Old Testament this is true for the books of Moses, the Psalms of David, the Wisdom of Solomon; in the intertestamental apocalyptic literature it is the case for the so-called apocalypse of Abraham, of Adam and of Daniel, of Moses or of the Twelve Patriarchs. In the New Testament too this phenomenon has clearly been applied. There is no one who now doubts that the second letter of Peter is a pseudepigraphical document dating from early in the second century, although the author represents himself as the apostle Peter. Thus again the problem is not as simple as it may seem at first to be. In the gospel of John a number of elements are present which cause serious doubt about whether the apostle himself – who according to Acts 4:13 is described as an unlettered and simple person, anything but an acquaintance of Annas or Caiaphas! – would have written with his own hand this elevated and impenetrably deep document.

We will limit ourselves to two elements of internal criticism. Firstly, the evangelist continually speaks of 'the Jews' (in Greek, *hoi ioudaioi;* John uses the word 71 times while the three synoptics together use it only 16 times). The Jews did not use this word to refer to themselves, it was the term that gentiles (Greeks, Romans, others) used to referred to the people. We are given the impression that the author of the gospel of John is quite distant from the Jews. He always speaks 'globally' about 'the Jews', and makes little if any distinction between the classes such as Pharisees and Sadducees. He always appears to be speaking as someone who does not consider himself a member of the people of Israel, but who rather is an outsider. Could he himself be believing Galilean Jew? See for example Jn 10:33-34. Jesus is again engaged in a controversy and says, 'Is it not written in your law, "I said, you are gods"?' Why does he speak of 'your' law? These seem to be words of an outsider discussing with the Jews. Can this not be an indication of the evangelist's identity?

Secondly, the gospel of John demonstrates a number of peculiarities which indicate that *it was not written all at once*. Chapter 21 has been added to the original ending of 20:30-31, and also the farewell discourse must have been composed in more than one phase. Chapter 14:31 seems to jar with 15:1 but fits perfectly with 18:1. In general, exegetes are of the opinion that chapters 15 to 17 were inserted at a later time in an already existing text. Would an author not have smoothed out such wrinkles in his own text?

On the other hand there are a number of elements in the gospel which point to very old and authentically Palestinian recollections. In its geographical and topographical references the gospel is often more exact than the synoptics, see 1:28; 3:23; 4:5-6; 11:18,54, etc. It shows that John is very familiar with the Palestinian situation of Jesus' time, for example, the tension between the Jews and Samaritans (4:9,20); the social customs (4:26); the liturgical and ritual customs (2:6; 3:25; 7:2,14,37; 11:55; 11:38,44; 18:28; 19:31) etc. This document is clearly based on unmistakably authentic Jesus tradition and knowledge of the Palestinian environment. John's gospel thus shows a strange mixture of alienation and familiarity regarding the original Palestinian Jesus tradition.

We can summarize the predominating opinion among biblical scholars on the authorship of the fourth gospel as follows: the gospel of John was probably *written in several stages*. It is quite possible that the preaching of 'the beloved disciple' forms the foundation of the material of the present gospel, but it is much less likely that he himself was the book's final editor. Internal criticism of the book seems to point more in the direction of an *editing by one or several disciples* after the death of the apostle, or at least of 'the beloved disciple'. One of these disciples of 'the beloved disciple' must have been the ingenious thinker and mystic who bestowed on the material from the preaching of the beloved disciple and on the other traditional material (possibly Mark?) its so typically 'Johannine' structure and tone.[6] Perhaps the disciple was the evangelist (i.e. the writer of the gospel); perhaps he only wrote some notes for the gospel and the editor who gave it definitive shape has to be sought elsewhere among the disciples of this brilliant thinker. This last could explain the gospel's 'broken' structure and the additions. Followers would have brought the original texts together and added later elements (such as chapter 21) to the original composition.

N.B. The grandiose prologue of the gospel also poses questions for investigators. In this prologue (Jn 1:1-18) the dominating term is Word (in Greek *Logos*). Christ is the divine *Logos* who has made the Father known to us. Christ is himself the incarnate Word! The reader of the prologue has the impression that 'the Word' will be the main theme of the gospel which follows. But surprisingly enough, the idea *Logos* is not used with this meaning anywhere else in the book, as is the case with the term 'grace' which is used four times in the prologue and is clearly emphasized there (1:14;16,17). Obviously, scholars have come to wonder about the origin of this prologue. Did the evangelist compose it as such for the gospel? Why then does the author not develop the themes of *Logos* or grace further? Was it originally a separate composition (according to many, a liturgical composition) which the author adapted as overture for his gospel (i.e. by including two references to John the Baptist 1:6-8,15)? Did the prologue belong to the gospel from the start or was it added later? The last words have not been spoken on these intriguing questions.

In sum, the author of the gospel of John can best be considered an anonymous Christian from 'the Johannine school', i.e. the group of disciples formed by the apostle (or at least by the 'beloved disciple'). The evangelist's followers have in their turn added elements (eventually from the evangelist's notes). This way of working – which we cannot prove compellingly – need not surprise us. We meet it often in the Old Testament. The books of Isaiah and Ezekiel were not written as such by the prophets themselves; the books are the end products of people from the 'school' of the prophets.

– Traditionally, Ephesus in Asia Minor is mentioned as the *place* of origin. Modern exegesis has also thought of the interior of Syria or even Egypt, since the gospel seems to have been widespread there at an early date. Yet Ephesus (where there were still followers of the Baptist and where John's Church is usually situated) remains the best candidate. As an important metropolis, Ephesus is an excellent focus for the various religious and philosophical movements which can be found in the gospel's background such as the Greek philosophical ideas from Platonism and Stoicism, mystery religions, far antecedents of gnosticism, etc. One intriguing mystery that still remains is the apparent total absence of contact with the Pauline community or with Pauline thought. The apostle to the gentiles had stayed a long period in Ephesus, and a flourishing Pauline community had grown in the city.

– The oldest known manuscript of the New Testament is the renowned 'Papyrus 52' from the John Rylands Library in Manchester. It is a minuscule scrap of papyrus, written on both sides and containing five (fragmentary) verses from the 18th chapter of John's gospel (vv. 31-33 and 37-38). Specialists date this papyrus, found in Egypt, as being written around the year 125. From this we know that John's gospel was already circulating – or at least was present – there by that time. We can thus accept that the gospel was written several years before this date. On the other hand, the text shows evidence of a great distance between Christians and Jews – far more than in the synoptics – and seems to refer to theological problems which can best be situated at the end of the first century. For this reason the most generally accepted *date* for the gospel of John lies between the years 95 and 100.

Specific characteristics of John's gospel

In this section we compile a number of characteristics which confer on the fourth gospel is particular colour and atmosphere. These characteristics relate in one way or another to the way of writing, to the author's style, but touch immediately on the document's content.

1. Despite some insertions and additions (see above) and despite a certain carelessness (compare for example 8:31 with 8:37 or 13:36 with 16:5 and note the contradiction), the whole of the fourth gospel has a more *closed composition* than do the synoptics. Where we readily notice in the first three gospels – especially in Mark – that the material originally consisted of numerous short scenes, short independent saying of Jesus and stories about Jesus which the evangelists, as it were, sewed together, this impression as good as disappears in John. In his gospel, the scenes are fewer in number and are related in long, continuous text units which we can no longer easily separate into smaller pericopes (see for example Jn 4; 5; 6; 9; 11). We no longer find short prophetic or doctrinal sayings of Jesus strung together, no disputes which end in a short clenched point, but long speeches and monologues or discussions (see 5:19-47; 6:29-59; 7-8; 13-17) form the largest part of the saying material. More than the other gospels, the gospel of John gives the impression of being a continuous book. The original mosaic of small, free standing traditional sayings and stories has been more thoroughly kneaded into a single unit.

This characteristic is also an argument for a later dating for the gospel. In John a further evolution in the treatment of the material of the gospel tradition can be noted revealing a later stage of editing. We could compare this with the evolution in nearly all branches of art. While the great compositions in gothic painting consist of a collection of small panels or scenes, the later artists constructed their largest canvases or frescos from one closed plan of composition; while the first oratoria and operas consisted of a string of several smaller 'numbers', the later composers will conceive of the most gigantic epics for the most part as a single whole; the older novels, such as Don

Quixote, consist of a series of short and more or less independent scenes, while later novelists will produce very comprehensive literary constructions conceived of as a single unit.

≥ We must also view the elimination of the 'pure' literary genres found in the other gospels or their absorption in larger units as an indication of a later stage of development. The subtle points contained in the stories or controversies (see Mk 2:15-28) are absorbed in John in long discussions and monologues. The most outstanding phenomenon in this regard is the omission of the real parable genre. The original – and surely historically related to Jesus – parable genre is, as it were, 'shrunk' in John to what are called 'I sayings', which all relate to the mystery of Jesus' person and which never formally speak of the kingdom of God. 'I am the bread of life... I am the good shepherd... I am the resurrection and the life...' See for example 6:48,51; 8:12; 10:7,9,11; 11:25; 14:6; 15:1. ≤

2. The greater unity and the closed composition are also abetted by a conspicuous *concentration of the theme*. The gospel of John has significantly fewer themes than the other gospels. In a certain way we could even say that there is only *one theme*, namely, *believing or not believing that Jesus is the Son, sent by the Father*. All the miracle stories or discussions turn as a spiral around this central theme. One could suggest, somewhat disrespectfully, that John is always harping on the same issue. The whole gospel is a series of variations on a single theme. We cannot deny that the gospel has a *monotonous character*. This is fostered by a rather *limited vocabulary* in which a number of key words are repeated frequently, words which support the theological theme (love; truth, light, life, judgement; world, witness; knowledge; the Father; be sent...). But John uses his limited vocabulary with great acuity. It must also be admitted that the evangelist with this monotony reaches a stately and poetic *grandeur* in which few are his equal! Think, for example, of the prologue or the farewell discourse. Whoever appreciates Gregorian music or icons, knows that monotony and intense beauty can coincide quite well. John's gospel is somewhat like Beethoven's Diabelli variations, we can never quite measure their depths. John is always writing the same thing, but he is

never merely repeating. He creates spirals around a centre which bring us ever deeper in his thoughts. There is only one theme, but it is inexhaustibly rich. The Johannine thematic concentration determines his whole theology.

≥ 3. The concentrated theme and the monotony do not mean that the author does not have a real narrative gift. His stories often reach the vitality of Mark's (read, for example, the healing of the one born blind, Jn 9, or the conversation with Pilate 18:28-19:16). But he attains this vitality and penetrating power primarily (and more than Mark) through a strong *sense of drama*. Many scenes from John's gospel are expressly dramatic in the etymological sense of the word they could easily be performed on a stage. There is, for example, the conversation with the Samaritan woman (Jn 4) where even a well placed 'change of scene' determines the structure of the story (see 4:6-7,8,27-28,31, 40). See also the long discussion in John 7-8, the healing of the one born blind (9), the scene with Pilate (18-19), the raising of Lazarus (11) and still more scenes. The gospel shows *in its whole a strong dramatic structure*, it is the story, or better the continuing drama of a protagonist (Jesus) in conflict with his antagonists or opponents (the Jews), in which the other figures – the disciples included – play the extras. Jesus remains the protagonist up to and including the moment he gives up his life and spirit (the Spirit?). In the background (we could almost say behind the curtains) is the Father, in whose name Jesus places his whole mission, an important dramatic role. ≤

≥ A typical stylistic device contributing to the drama is what is called *Johannine irony*. This is an expression with a 'false bottom'. On one level, it is the conversation of different people with Jesus, they do not understand him and Jesus uses this lack of understanding to drive the conversation higher and higher. A second level is that of the relationship between the evangelist and his reader, between the lines the evangelist 'winks', as it were, to attract the reader's attention to the deeper meaning lying behind Jesus' words. John warns his readers, 'watch out there is more here than what there seems!' Examples of Johannine irony can be found in 3:3-4; 4:10-15; 6:41; 7:33-35; 9:29-30; 11:49-50; 19:19-22. This device is closely related to Johannine symbolism, for example in 9:7, Jesus said 'to him, "Go, wash in the pool of Siloam" (which means Sent). So he went and washed and came back seeing.' The apparent aside to benefit those who understood no Hebrew explaining the 'translation' of 'Siloam' – 'the sent' – seems unimportant and merely informative. In reality it has a very important function in the story of the one born blind. Here we are given the key to understand the whole story, namely, if someone born blind – and who is not? – wants to see, then he has to wash his eyes in the One Sent, i.e. in Christ himself! ≤

4. In addition to its dramatic character, the gospel also has a certain *polemical character*. The term 'the Jews' often has a really polemical echo, and we discover practically throughout the whole gospel an underlying assault on 'those who will not believe'. Many commentators have pointed out that John gives the impression of wanting to *reopen the trial against Jesus*, to expose the Jews' error and to demonstrate the Jesus was innocent and was sent by God. To reach this goal, he calls upon *witnesses* from early on in his gospel who testify in Jesus' defence. 'Witnessing' is one of the central concepts of John's gospel. And the witnesses are numerous: John the Baptist, the Scriptures (Moses!), the signs, the Samaritan woman, the lame, the one born blind, Pilate, the beloved disciple and above all the Father himself.

5. We will not go into detail here on the *symbolism* aspect of John's gospel, but refer back to the discussion of it in chapter 2 (see above pp. 41 ff) where we discussed history as symbol. We had said that our vision was inspired by Sandra Schneiders' article on the gospel of John. What is said there of the four gospels is especially true of the fourth.

Whoever wants to understand John's gospel may not remain fixated on the level of storytelling. In this gospel we often find a symbolic dimension under the words and events. By this we mean that John tends to highlight the facts of Jesus' life – in particular his miracles – in terms of their spiritual meaning. That is why the miracles are called 'signs', and he himself says that there are witnesses to the miracles who have not seen the signs. See Jn 6:26. The events are not important on their own, but only because they give shape to a deeper mystery. Symbolism is everywhere: Nathanael under the fig tree (1:48); water into wine in Cana (2:1-11); water in the story of the Samaritan woman (4); the washing of the feet (13:1-17); 'and it was night...' (13:30); the seamless garment (19:23b-24); blood and water from Jesus' side (19:34); etc.

In John's gospel, symbolism is not only related to individual words or stories. It buttresses the whole of his gospel. This has important consequences for the relationship between historicity and symbolism. Here the historical basis of symbolism is not the related events or words as such, but rather *the historical Jesus event as a whole.* Or put differently, *Jesus himself with the facts of his presence and his personal history, are the indelible historical basis of Johannine symbolism.* The evangelist often represents this transparency of the historical Jesus as 'symbol of God' (see pp. 42 ff) in stories which as such 'did not really happen', or in words which 'were not really spoken', but which express the profound dimension of the historical Jesus. Among such purely symbolic stories belong the changing of water into wine at the marriage at Cana. Jesus himself is the true wine of the marriage feast, the good wine of the messianic time. It is not the related events that form the historical basis of the miracle – although there could be recollections here of a marriage feast where Jesus was present with his mother and his disciples – but the totality of Jesus' historical person. In word and deed, it 'revealed his glory' as the new wine of God's Way, better than the first wine of the Old Covenant. An excellent example of one of Jesus' 'purely symbolic speeches' is the profound farewell discourse in which John has Jesus articulate the ripe fruit of his meditation on the mystery of Christ as his testament to the Church.

Main theological themes of John's gospel

It has been said countless times that John himself formulated the theological intentions of his gospel, and this in the original conclusion to the book, 20:30-31, 'Now Jesus did many other signs in the presence of the disciples, which are not written in this book; but these are written *that you may believe that Jesus is the Christ, the Son of God, and that believing you may have life in his name.*' We have no doubt that it is indeed there that we must look for the main purpose of the gospel. The two-fold nature of the purpose is immediately apparent. There is first a *christological* purpose: Jesus is the Christ the Son of God. And secondly there is a *soteriological* purpose: the believer will have life in his name. (Note 'soteriology' means teaching about salvation; soteriological thus means what relates to salvation or the teaching about salvation, to redemption or the teaching about redemption.) The two theological pronouncements (Jesus is the Son of God / you may have life in his name) are held together by the *faith*. The book is written so that we may *believe* that Jesus is the Christ, and *through this believing* have life in his name. In a certain sense we could apply to the gospel of John, Paul's great principle that humanity is saved by faith.

Of course – and we have written it several times – this conclusion to John's gospel puts into words the purpose of *every* gospel. That is why we have to look at the traits that characterize the *specifically Johannine* development of this fundamental intention.

Christological concentration

All the gospels are christologically oriented. The reader is invited to confess that Jesus of Nazareth is the Christ (= the Anointed, the Messiah). In the synoptics the christological theme is linked to other themes, referring to recollections of *the content of Jesus' message.* We hear a Jesus who does not so much proclaim about himself or explicitly declare himself Messiah, but rather preaches about the coming of the kingdom of God breaking through in his activity. Jesus preaches the kingdom of God and gives it a specific content. We learn of how he sees that kingdom in his parables, in his controversies on the Law, in his behaviour to the sick, the rejected and to sinners. We learn of the way of life necessary to enter the kingdom of God (or about life as part of the kingdom of God) from the sermon on the mount or the ecclesiastical discourse in Matthew or the sermon on the plain in Luke.

That Jesus is the Christ, certainly belongs to the synoptic's *formal* (their intended) point of view. But the question of whether or not he is the Messiah does not have the most important *material* place in the first three gospels (it is only very explicit in Peter's confession, the confession of the evil spirits, Caiaphas' question, the ridicule at the cross and the centurion's confession after Jesus' death). The gospel stories' attention is materially more centred on the content of Jesus' words (the preaching of the kingdom of God), on his deeds and on the (discordant) events surrounding him. The confession about Christ to which the gospels lead must be the result of the whole story.

In John's gospel the focus of attention is clearly elsewhere. The formal goal of a gospel, namely, showing that Jesus is the Messiah has become for him also *the material content* of his text. In other words, John writes his whole gospel story directly around the question of whether or not Jesus is the Son of God and whether or not we should believe him. Whoever should ask, on the basis of John's gospel, what Jesus' message is, would not really come to learn much more than that, 'I am the Son of God. Believe in Me'. The gospel is far less focused on the content of Jesus' message than around the express question whether this message is or is not the message of the Son of God. *What* he as Son of God had to say is apparently of far less importance to John's gospel than the affirmation *that* he speaks as Son of God. The gospel of John has correctly been called a *christological reduction* of the theme.

In reading it we receive the definite impression that everything in John's gospel is shifted. The parables have become Messianic self-affirmations (the 'I sayings'); the controversies no longer involve points of the Law or their interpretation but directly the question of whether or not Jesus is the Son of God (e.g. chapters 7-8); the signs turn into monologues or dramatically constructed dialogues whose object is demonstrating that Jesus is the Son of God and the One Sent by the Father; even the meetings (Nathanael, Nicodemus, the Samaritan woman,

Pilate…) are thematically written in function of the question of Jesus' identity. In short, the original gospel genres (as form criticism has identified them) have, in John's gospel, all undergone an evolution in function of the one, dominating question: *is Jesus or is he not the Son of God?* Given this, we must not be surprised that we find in John's gospel the 'highest' christological expressions about Jesus. The prologue is there to prove that John's reflection on the person of Jesus and on the essence of his mission have led to a very daring, very far-reaching 'christology from above', in which Jesus Christ is placed radically in the heart of the eternal God and is attributed with divine status.

John's christological reduction is also one of the aspects of his gospel which allow us to presuppose that the evangelist in all probability handled the material he received from tradition *very creatively*. The sayings of Jesus in the fourth gospel do not (or only slightly) reflect Jesus of Nazareth's own historical manner of speaking, but rather the Johannine concentration of all the gospel material around the all-dominating question of whether of not Jesus was the Son of God.

John's christological concern fits remarkably well in a gospel that wants to reopen *Jesus' trial* against those who have answered this question negatively. The evangelist 'digs up the file', as it were, and reissues subpoenas to all the witnesses to support the assertion that Jesus' claims were indeed well founded. The almost hectic compulsion to show that Jesus is the Son of God, added to the reopening of the 'trial', have led a number of researchers to ask whether or not John's gospel was intended only for Christians. It occasionally sounds as if the evangelist wants to convince non-Christians (Jews?). There is not much that can be said with certainty, but if any of the gospels is to be thought suited to fulfil an apologetic function toward 'outsiders' then John is certainly the best candidate.

To these considerations, one more can be added. Since John makes the formal christological question the almost exclusive material content of his gospel, should we not ask whether the evangelist did not write for people who already knew the other gospels? What the rest of Jesus' message might have been and how Christians are to live in a community cannot be gleaned from the fourth gospel. The Christians who followed Paul had no gospel book, but Paul gave them directions on the central points of faith (resurrection, eucharist, ultimate expectations...) and especially concrete Christian ethics.

In any case, we can agree completely with the remarks on Johannine ecclesiology Herman Ridderbos wrote in 1987 in his commentary on John:

What marks the fourth gospel and gives it its special character is... the tremendous *reduction* which he applies as editor on *all the rest of the material* (which he could have written) on behalf of the *one point* on which he wants to concentrate all his readers' attention, namely, on *the person and identity* of Jesus Christ, the Son of God and on believing in *his* name, 20:30-31. Perhaps we may, for this reason, say that the fourth gospel, given the way and the degree to which it applies this concentration and reduction, is a very unique representative of the 'genre' gospel, modifying it such that we may consider it the last phase in the development of the phenomenon 'gospel'. It is primarily because of this concentration on one point, giving the fourth gospel a strongly 'interpretive' character, that many scholars believe that we can no longer discover the original eye-witness but only the later 'charismatic' or 'theologian'. Of course, we can say of all the gospels' writers that they are not merely collectors but 'evangelists' in the full sense of the word, concerned not only with passing on historical knowledge about Jesus but above all with inflaming and strengthening 'faith in his name', working on this basis, each in his own way, to edit the writings. But while *the synoptic authors* as evangelists exerted all efforts for the advancement and richness of the tradition, to put its saving message in front of their readers, in the fourth gospel the priority for a large part lies in the direct and express *interpretation* of this knowledge, and its author gives *descriptive* history a much more consciously subservient role than is the case with the synoptic authors.

We see this immediately in the way he precedes his gospel story with the prologue in which he shows in a fundamental and clear way in what light he has understood 'the life of Jesus' and how he wants his readers to understand it, namely, as the incarnation of the Word, who in the beginning was with God, and who was God. What is postulated in the prologue not only forms the 'theological' *plan* but also determines the *structure* of the gospel story and the *criterion* for what the evangelist in his writing considers necessary and sufficient – leaving aside the rest of the material – for leading his readers to and strengthening them in the belief that Jesus is the Christ, the Son of God. Even when he calls upon much broader knowledge than that he may safely presume his readers possess (such as the extensive reference to Jesus' activities outside Galilee), he is still not concerned with adding something to what he does presume they already know, but only with that one point around which even the smallest details are situated.'[7]

In conclusion we must say that John's christological concentration also determines the *theological chronology* of his gospel. The revelation of Jesus' glory occurs, as it were, in two phases. His active period in called *The Day* (see Jn 9:4), it is the period when he 'works', i.e. reveals his true essence in words and signs and prepares the moment when he will be glorified. But the definitive revelation of his mission by the Father, and thus his glorification as Son of God, takes place in the Easter event (the triptych death - resurrection - ascension). This central moment is called *The Hour* (Jn 2:4; 7:30; 8:20; 12:23). In John's gospel the 'Day' extends from chapter 1 to chapter 12; the 'Hour' covers chapters 13 to 20.

*Soteriology (view of salvation) and eschatology
(view of the last days)*

 – The *teaching on salvation* found in John's gospel follows logically the flow of his christological concentration. John emphasizes heavily the question of humanity's salvation. The gospel is written so that people 'will have life', i.e. will participate in salvation. Jesus is the saviour of the world (4:42); he is light, way, truth, life (8:12; 14:6); he conquers the world of unbelief and evil (12:31; 16:33). In John, the question of salvation no longer takes the shape of the alternative 'Jew or gentile', but is thought of *universally*, i.e. as light. Jesus is the salvation of the whole world, for all people trapped in darkness.

The Johannine teaching on salvation is – can it be otherwise? – *concentrated completely on christology*. Jesus Christ himself *is* the salvation of the world; this is the reason for the abundance of 'I sayings' in which the attainment of salvation is tightly linked to the person of Jesus, to his identity as Son of God. John no longer speaks thematically of the kingdom of God (in contrast to the synoptics – and Jesus himself – for whom 'salvation' was the equivalent of 'being part of, entering into the kingdom of God'), because for him the kingdom of God, as it were, coincides with the person of Jesus. We could almost say that Jesus Christ himself is the kingdom of God. Entering into the kingdom comes to mean community with Christ, where we immediately meet the *mystical* dimension of John's gospel (see especially 15:1-11, see also John's ecclesiology or view of the Church, below). This approach also sheds light on the fact that in John's gospel Jesus uses all these expressions which no longer say that he *brings* the Way to God or Life, but that he *is* both salvation and the way to it. Expressions such as 'I am the Way, the Truth and the Life' can only be understood through the christological reduction within the Johannine view on salvation.

– It is obvious that the mystical association betweensalvation and the person of Jesus will also be felt in John's *eschatology*.[8]

Within the framework of Luke's gospel (see above, p. 161 f) we already mentioned the problems the early Christians had with the final days. The expectation of salvation and the final days always (even today) is found in the area of tension between 'the already' and 'the not yet', the 'present' and the 'future'. When can we say a person has entered salvation? Here, where he believes and loves, and gives shape to his love and justice? Or later, in the 'hereafter' or at the 'end of time'? What is the relationship between salvation's 'here and now' and its future dimension?

Luke found an element of the solution by 'creating' Church history. In John's gospel, we have the impression that the tension between the 'already' and the 'not yet' is released to a certain degree by suggesting that salvation ('eternal life') is already present when one listens to and believes in Jesus Christ. The English exegete Charles Harold Dodd has strongly insisted on John's *realized eschatology*. The gospel of John has without doubt also greatly influenced another eminent theologian and exegete, Rudolf Bultmann, who wrote a brilliant – if very subjective – commentary on John's gospel. Bultmann has developed a strongly 'existential' interpretation of the resurrection which can be summarized as follows. Where people believe, i.e. where they are converted to God by Christ's Word, *there* is the resurrection for these people. Resurrection is thus essentially an existential reality, one taking place here and now in our existence, where people leave their darkness and become believers. In other words, Bultmann no longer sees salvation (for resurrection and salvation are, for him, almost synonymous) as something in the future, but something present now in the very act of faith.

John has a number of texts which favours such an interpretation. Bultmann has put them in the spotlight. The texts in question are especially 5:24-25 and 6:47. 'Truly, truly, I say to you, he who hears my word and believes him who sent me, has eternal life; he does not come into judgement, but has passed from death to life...' In our opinion it is undeniable that we meet in John a sort of 'realized eschatology'. He sees a person's eschatological expectations already fulfilled in his believing existence. This point is also easy to understand when we think of John's christological reduction. Salvation and the expectation of salvation are necessarily related to eschatological reality, i.e. with the ultimate purpose of our lives. It is also true that Christians refer to the ultimate goal and completion of salvation as 'resurrection'. Where people are risen, they realize their ultimate and definitive saving reality, i.e. life in (with) God. If in John belief in Jesus already means that believers have entered into salvation (John's view of salvation), then the next step to an eschatology realized here and now is very small. Where some-one believes that Jesus is the Son of God, there dawns his *eschaton*, his definitive saving reality. In this sense *someone who has come to believe has already risen from the dead. Whoever believes in Jesus has already risen.*

Does this mean that John abandoned every expectation of future salvation? Has he eliminated the 'not yet'? We do not think so? Bultmann has interpreted John too one-sidedly in function of his own theological conviction. There are also enough texts to be found in John which refer to a resurrection on 'the last day' where the context does not allow us to say that he considers 'the last day' to be the day when a person comes to believe. Bultmann thought such passages came from someone else that the original evangelist. We find a peculiar mixture of present and future in John's gospel when he speaks of resurrec-tion and eternal life. See 5:25-29:

> Truly, truly, I say to you, the hour is coming, and now is, when the dead will hear the voice of the Son of God, and whose who hear will live. For as the Father has life in himself, so he granted the Son also to have life in himself, and has given him authority to execute judgement, because he is the Son of man. Do not marvel at this; for the hour is coming when all who are in the tombs will hear his voice and come forth, those who have done good, to the resurrection of life, and those who have done evil, to the resurrection of judgement.

See also 6:40-47,51-18; 11:23-27.

John's view of the Church or ecclesiology

Under this heading we gather together a few short remarks on the life of believers as Christian community.

For John, too, being Christian is being Church. Being Church is essentially being part of Christ as the tendrils are part of the grape vine (15:1ff). Being Church, as being believers together, is supported by a *mystical* dimension. Christians are joined together and form a Church when they remain 'in' Christ. The link with Christ is not present when belief refers to a mere mental agreement. Put differently, that a person believes Jesus is the Christ must be visible in concrete attitudes and behaviour. We must live before Jesus as Jesus lives before the Father, i.e. in obedience to his commandments. The commandments are summarized in *one commandment of love*.

Here we see that for John, the word commandment has no negative association at all. 'Commandment' will only say 'God's will' realized in concrete actions. But God's will is exclusively love, and love is directed toward liberation. For John – just as for Paul, and in a line with the exodus tradition and the Ten Commandments – God's commandments are nothing other than concrete paths to freedom. Commandments which would no longer serve freedom, could not possibly be God's commandments, for they do not express his will. As Jesus fulfils the Father's will, so must the believer also fulfil the Father's will; as Jesus has loved – unto death – so must believers love. Love and mutual unity are the signs that someone is a follower of Christ. The farewell discourse must be read in this sense. Jesus said, 'If a man loves me, he will keep my word... He who does not love me does not keep my words...' (14:23-24). And also, 'This is my commandment, that you love one another as I have loved you. Greater love has no man than this, that a man lay down his life for his friends. You are my friends if you do what I command you' (15:12-17). See also 17:20-26 where the unity among the disciples is the sign of their belonging to Christ. This is the *ethic* of John's gospel. We have already mentioned the fact that the Johannine ethic is not preoccupied with concrete cases. This too is the result of the christological reduction. Christian morality is nothing other than being to one another and to God as Jesus, even 'in' the glorious Lord who remains present through the Holy Spirit (the 'paraclete' or 'recourse'). It is the Spirit who will keep reminding us of his message and help us to understand it (cf 14:25; 16:5-15). Christian (Church) ethics is for John to go in freedom along the way Jesus went – in love unto death!

The concreteness of this love is very heavily emphasized in the first letter of John, another important document of the Johannine school. We have the impression that Jesus' farewell discourse in the gospel touches the theme which will be so explicitly developed in 1 John, namely, that believing is not merely mentally endorsing or 'knowing' (gnosis!) the message, but presupposes essentially a believing 'practice' or 'ethic'. A person is a believer only when he *acts* like one, i.e. when he stands in the world as Jesus stood, in love *put into practice*. The Holy Spirit is only present where people *live according to* Jesus' word. Then only do they glorify Jesus, cf 14:15-17. Read also the magnificent texts in 1 John 3:11-24; 4:7-5:4. They are written under the motto that whoever says he loves God but hates his brother is a liar. In 1 John the eschatological expectation of salvation is already present in the one who loves his brother, 'We know that we have passed out of death into life, because we love the brethren. He who does not love abides in death' (3:14). This is a magnificent unity. In the gospel people rise from the dead by believing, by listening to the word of the Son. But believing is loving as Jesus loved, and thus whoever loves his brother has passed from death to life.

There is much discussion on the role of the *sacraments* in John's gospel. On the one side is Rudolf Bultmann's extreme thesis which asserts that John's gospel is written from an anti-sacramental tendency. On the other is the extreme position of Oscar Cullmann who gives the whole gospel a sacramental interpretation. It is remarkable that John omits both Jesus' baptism and the institution of the eucharist. But it is difficult to find any other than a sacramental interpretation of such verses as Jn 3:5 (born of water and the spirit), 6:48-58 (who eats my flesh and drinks my blood) and 19:34 (blood and water from the side of the crucified Christ), i.e. to interpret them as anything other than references to *baptism* and *eucharist*. Personally we prefer C. K. Barrett's interpretation. He believes that John accepts the sacraments but adopts a critical stance to avoid their being understood as semi-magical means to salvation in themselves, analogous to what was happening at that time in the mystery religions. Later devotional Church customs have abundantly demonstrated that the danger of a magical interpretation of the sacraments is never far off!

As with Matthew and Luke, missionary activity is important in John's view of the Church. John has apparently outgrown the difficult problem of 'Jews or gentiles' (note that this is another argument for the gospel's late date). For him the missionary task is completely universal, see 4:38ff; 10:16; 11:52; 17:18; 20:21. The mission is directed toward the whole world. A remarkable text in this regard is Jn 12:20-36 on the mysterious meeting with the Greeks. The scene takes place at the end of Jesus' public life, just before the start of the passion. Among the pilgrims going to Jerusalem, there are also a few Greeks, gentiles. They want to speak to Jesus and therefore attach themselves to Philip. When Philip and Andrew take this message to Jesus, he answers abruptly, 'The hour has come for the Son of man to be glorified. Truly, truly, I say to you, unless a grain of wheat falls into the earth and dies, it remains alone; but if it dies, it bears much fruit' (12:23-24). The Greek's attempt to approach Jesus ushers in the hour of his glorification. It is difficult not to see a reference here to the mission to the gentiles. The crucified Jesus is glorified by the entrance of the gentiles into the community of believers. When Jesus will be lifted up from the earth – in John this means crucified and glorified and even more, glorified in the cross – he will draw all to himself (12:32). The whole world. For God is the God of all, and all who want to come to Christ come to the Father. It is no accident that Jesus' 'Day' ends with the words:

He who believes in me, believes not in me but in him who sent me. And he who sees me sees him who sent me. I have come as light into the world, that whoever believes in me may not remain in darkness. If any one hears my sayings and does not keep them, I do not judge him; for I did not come to judge the world but to save the world. He who rejects me and does not receive my sayings has a judge; the word that I have spoken will be his judge on the last day. For I have not spoken on my own authority; the Father who sent me has himself given me commandment what to say and what to speak. And I know that his commandment is eternal life. What I say, therefore, I say as the Father has bidden me.

And this is what the Hour will reveal to the salvation of the whole world: the unity of the Father and the Son.

NOTES

1   D. Mollat, *Evangile de Saint-Jean* [*The Gospel of Saint John*], DDB, 1960 p. 44.
2   A. Lemmers, 'Johannes (Evangelie)' [John (Gospel of)] in *Bijbels Woordenboek* [*Biblical Dictionary*], 3rd ed., Roermond - Maaseik, 1966-69, col. 722.
3   Among them C. H. Dodd, R. Schnackenburg, R. Brown, J. Becker, S. Smalley, S. Schulz, R. Bultmann and H. Van Den Bussche.
4   Especially F. Neirynck (Leuven) defends this thesis with impressive arguments. But other authors such as C. K. Barrett, W. G. Kümmel, B. Lindars and M. E. Boismard also think along the same lines, even if using other arguments.
5   R. Schnackenburg, *Das Johannesevangelium* [*The Gospel of John*] HTKNT IV, vol. 1 Freiburg, 1965, pp. 60ff; vol. 3, ibid, 1975, p. 461. R. Brown, *The Gospel according to John*, AB 29, NY: Doubleday, 1966, vol 1, pp. LXXXII ff; id. *The Community of the Beloved Disciple*, op. cit., pp. 33f; see also J. Colson, *L'énigme du disciple que Jésus aimait* [*The enigma of the beloved disciple*], Paris, 1969, who also defends the position that the disciple was a Jerusalemite and not an apostle.
6   This could lead to some confusion in the terminology. When the exegetes speak of 'typically Johannine' they do not mean coming from the apostle John, the son of Zebedee, but rather, having the same linguistic and stylistic features as the gospel of John, which may not have been written by the apostle.
7   H. N. Ridderbos, *Het Evangelie naar Johannes. Proeve van een theologische exegese* [*The Gospel of John. Attempt at a Theological Exegesis*], vol. I, Kampen, 1987, p. 17f.
8   Our word 'eschatology' comes from the Greek *ton eschaton* or *ta eschata* which means 'the last things, the end, what comes at the end'. Eschatology comprises all that has to do with humanity's final expectations, with the way in which it sees the ultimate, definitive realization of its existence. Eschatology is the pre-eminent terrain of the believers, *hope* directed toward the final, the definitive (we speak also of 'ultimate') reality.